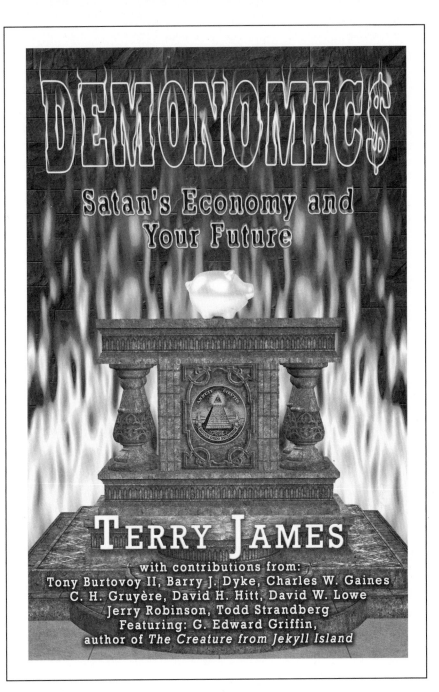

# DEMONOMICS

## Satan's Economy and Your Future

# TERRY JAMES

with contributions from:
Tony Burtovoy II, Barry J. Dyke, Charles W. Gaines
C. H. Gruyère, David H. Hitt, David W. Lowe
Jerry Robinson, Todd Strandberg
Featuring: G. Edward Griffin,
author of *The Creature from Jekyll Island*

DEFENDER

CRANE, MISSOURI

Demonomics: Satan's Economy and Your Future
Defender
Crane, Missouri 65633
©2011 by Terry James
All rights reserved. Published 2011.
Printed in the United States of America.
ISBN: 978-0-9846300-7-3
ISBN: 0984 630074

A CIP catalog record of this book is available from the Library
of Congress.

Cover illustration and design by Shim Franklin.

Scripture quoted is taken from the King James Version.

# CONTENTS

# FOREWORD

*By David H. Hitt*

Each of us carries in our pockets a most powerful and curious item—money. We use it every day. From an early age, we are taught that we need money in order to function in a modern society. Needing money is not an option; it is a matter of survival, essentially on a par with air and water. This need pervades our lives, yet hardly anyone ever stops to ask what money really is and why we use it.

If you have a piece of currency handy, take a look at it. It certainly looks impresssive. The paper is heavy and strong, and has a rich texture. The artwork is of the finest quality. The words are official and important. Coins convey the same import; everything about them says, "Pay attention to me! I'm valuable!"

And we respond accordingly: We accumulate money. We care about how hard it works for us, and we think about where to move it to make it work even harder. We derive peace and comfort from knowing we have it. We celebrate its gain and fear its loss. We occasionally use it to measure ourselves against other people and then derive our esteem from it. Some of us design our lives around it. Others are even willing to lie and steal to get more of it.

All of this for a fancy piece of paper or a metal disk.

Is this all that money is? Or, does this stuff instead have more to do with what it represents and what it can buy for us? That question is more difficult and subtle than it first appears, as you will see.

It is also worth contemplating the size and complexity of the systems that are in place to support money: the mints, the banks, the stock exchanges, the machines, the secure boxes, and the alarms, just to name a few.

Then, assuming you are a Bible-believing Christian, you have to wonder about the role money plays in God's plan for mankind. First Timothy 6:10 famously tells us that the love of money is the root of all evil (and promises sorrow to those who love it). Matthew 27:3 recounts how Judas betrayed Jesus for a mere thirty pieces of silver. This was the same Jesus who threw the money changers out of the temple in John 2:15.

Looking into the future, Revelation 13:17 tells us that some kind of mark on our bodies will actually determine whether we are able to buy or sell. Then there are all those verses in Revelation 18 that talk about the merchants who profit from the Great Whore of Babylon and the intense agony they feel as they witness her destruction.

What is this all about? Could the money we are using today be leading to that end? Do we own our money—or does it, just maybe, own us?

Lots of secular books out there address history, money, banking, politics, economics, stocks, bonds, commodities, etc. The world doesn't really need another one of those, and this book makes no effort to be one. What Terry James has designed this book to do, instead, is lend biblical perspective to our economic reality—showing us how we can live in this financial world without losing our souls to it. He has assembled a terrific lineup of contributing authors who, each in his own way, will take you on a journey in which you will encounter many fascinating concepts. After reading this book, you may never look at that paper or metal in your pocket the same way again.

# ACKNOWLEDGMENTS

M Y MANY THANKS to each of the authors of this book for their generous willingness to share their vast knowledge of monetary matters. They are not only brilliant in their acumen and presentations, but make understandable the complexities of economics that otherwise are for the most part—to me, at least—incomprehensible.

My most profound thanks to David Hitt, who sparked the thought to bring into being such a timely volume. The concept is his from cover to cover, and I'm grateful beyond measure.

To Todd Strandberg, my www. raptureready.com partner and family-close friend, who came up with the title of *Demonomics*, and who daily amazes and amuses me with his Internet genius, my heartfelt thanks.

To Margaret, Terry, Jr., Nathan, Jeanie, and Kit—my love and thanks for putting up with me.

To my "daughters"—Dana, my superb research assistant, and Angie, the very best editor on the planet—my deep love and my thanks.

Thanks again to Tom and Nita Horn for finding this effort worthy of publication.

My gratitude to you, the reader, for whom this book will hopefully provide encouragement and help to move through the questionable economic times that likely lie just ahead.

Finally, to my Lord, Jesus Christ, my most humble thankfulness for all He has done and continues to do for me.

—Terry James

$

# INTRODUCTION

*By Terry James*

THIS IS THE book that will begin helping you understand the tumultuous monetary madness that holds captive every person on planet earth. America and the world are being rushed headlong into uncharted socioeconomic waters. Unprecedented, tsunami-like fiscal pressures gush at sovereign national currency structures, the flood bulldozing everything in its path toward a totally changed order of some sort.

No matter how the turbulence is examined, dissected, and/or analyzed, the ultimate destination at which the carnage is likely to arrive looks ominous from the perspectives of the authors of this book.

There is a force generating and pushing the tidal wave, some diabolist energy that manipulates and maneuvers behind the stage of history upon which mankind acts and reacts. We call this force "demonomics" in this book for the purpose of giving that force a face—a face behind which lurks an evil intention to bring all peoples of earth under absolute control.

It is an ancient evil that more often than not throughout the ages has acted insidiously rather than overtly. Its *modus operandi* of late, however, manifests aggression unlike at any time in man's history.

That is not to say the evil hasn't inflicted as much, or even more horrific, damage in the past. It is just that this force now is using heretofore unmatched methodology in exerting its determination to achieve a new world order.

The authors of *Demonomics* go behind the mask that is the face of the ancient evil. Each contributor expertly removes layer after layer from the deceptive façade presented by the malevolence. Each also lays out the evidence in real-world terminology, making the case that the present global financial system is on the brink of profound transformation and giving insights into what that change might mean for the reader.

## Personal Testimonial

My own knowledge of the complexities involved in micro and macro-economics was quite limited. I say *was* limited, because the scope of my understanding of the intricately intermeshed elements within economics has been vaulted to…well, I must be honest and tell you that I am still at a level of understanding that leaves much knowledge to be gained. But, I must also tell you that while working as general editor of this volume, my understanding has been given the economics education equivalent of a B-12 injection.

While reading each chapter, insight after insight pulsed within the part of my gray matter admittedly long deprived of study in the realm of economics. The lights came on, the illumination at times absolutely dazzling. It is surprising how facing the dark, ominous surroundings of uncertain times with the light of truth fortifies for facing one's future.

One example: In college days, sitting around the tables in student unions, we engaged in the youth-pretentious debates of the causes and effects of, for instance, war and peace. We most often concluded that somebody was getting rich off of the blood we—this was the era of the draft when Lyndon Johnson's Vietnam War was just revving up—were commanded to spill by the old-men politicians.

I wish I had, during those moments of opportunity for demonstrating erudition, been able to interject the instantly enlightening insight from G. Edward Griffin, in his chapter offering a look at the Federal Reserve System:

> The ancient alchemists sought in vain to convert lead into gold. Modern alchemists have succeeded in that quest. The lead bullets of war have yielded an endless source of gold for those magicians who create money out of thin air. The startling fact emerges that, without the ability to create fiat money, most modern wars simply would not have occurred. As long as this is allowed to function, future wars are inevitable.

Then, using the same author's words, I could have further wowed 'em with an Aristotelian syllogism, explaining the causes and effects of those war-and-peace matters made famous by Tolstoy, as we *intellectuals* sat around the student union tables:

A study of these and similar events reveals a personality profile not just of the Rothschilds, but of that special breed of international financiers whose success typically is built upon certain character traits. Those include cold objectivity, immunity to patriotism, and indifference to the human condition. That profile is the basis for proposing a theoretical strategy called the Rothschild Formula, which motivates such men to propel governments into war for the profits they yield. The Formula most likely has never been consciously phrased as it appears here, but subconscious motivations and personality traits work together to implement it nevertheless. As long as the mechanism of central banking exists, it will be to such men an irresistible temptation to convert debt into perpetual war and war into perpetual debt.

To have been able to parrot such insight, however, would have required that I knew what the terms like "fiat money" and "central banking" mean, and I would have had to explain the term "Rothschild Formula"—neither of which I was prepared to do, believe me.

Had I access to the insights that reside within these chapters, I could have known and forewarned my young peers of the luciferic malignity that would plague their futures, regurgitating the words of another *Demonomics* author, Charles W. Gaines, concerning central banks (in chapter three):

One thing is indisputably clear: The Federal Reserve, as is the case with, if not all, central banks, has the unfettered authority to print as much fiat money as it wants. This gives central banks significant control over economies and money supply, and it is by this mechanism that central banks can create inflation and boom-and-bust economic cycles, which in turn can be used to transfer wealth from the masses to a select few. For example, in the United States, purportedly under 1 percent of the population currently claims ownership to almost 50 percent of the wealth. This is a disturbing statistic, and unfortunately one that most likely will only continue to get worse.

There we go again with the economic speak. Boom-and-bust cycles! Don't worry; you will soon become an authority on what all of this means...

Now, at an age older even than the "old men" who were about to send us off to spill our blood back there in the early 1960s, I am fully prepared not only to use these terms, but to explain them. My cerebral quiver is full of even more complex economic words and terminology. The authors of *Demonomics* have taught them to me, and in ways that are easy to understand.

The exercise of learning about the evil economic dynamics that have brought America and the world to this precarious position in history was far from a painful process. It has been stimulating, even exhilarating. Most of all, it has been enlightening to the point that it has dispelled the foreboding that otherwise would darken all hope for the future.

This is a volume that does much, much more than cover historical financial treachery by the lords of finance. It moves far beyond mere explanations and definitions of terms—beyond dire forecasts of things to come. *Demonomics: Satan's Economy and Your Future* presents specific, practical advice on how to financially manage your way through difficult economic days that loom on the horizon. More than giving down-to-earth guidance through hard economic times, however, this is a volume that has at its center comforting biblical counsel, given mankind by the ultimate economist, the Creator of all things good.

chapter one

# GOD'S ECONOMY
*Real Money and Wealth Stewardship*

*By David W. Lowe*

A S ONE WHO has grown up in the United States of America, I've known only one type of economic system: capitalism, featuring the pursuit of wealth to obtain the American dream. I'm sure many reading this book are in the same camp. Under this system, we are shaped and groomed to follow its rules from birth to the grave. Have you ever stopped to contemplate this cycle?

At birth, you were assigned a Social Security number that serves as your identity in the system for your entire life. Then, if you were like most children, you entered the public education system, where you remained until your late teen years. This education was a social experiment and indoctrination in the ways of the secular world, including economic theory. The next step in the cycle was probably college and possibly graduate school, where your education continued and dreams of getting that perfect job began to come into focus.

Out of college—and perhaps after finding a soul mate with whom to share your life in matrimony—you then joined the rat race, becoming one of the millions who climb into the hamster wheel of professional life. Major components of the American dream, of course, are owning your own home and having at least two cars. For most, that entails becoming indebted with loans and a thirty-year mortgage. This is where you, dear hamster, must really start moving in earnest on that wheel, because in order to make those monthly payments, you must be gainfully employed.

As your career progresses, you begin to depend on insurance—health, automobile, home, and life—just in case something really bad happens. You also begin to rely on the retirement "carrot" that seems so far in the distance, but that comes more clearly into focus with each passing day. Along the way, you judiciously guard and massage your investments, such as a 401(k) retirement account, pensions, and individual retirement accounts, with the goal of attaining a certain level of wealth when you finally reach those golden years.

After decades of hard work and dedication, retirement eventually arrives, and it's time to enjoy the fruits of your labor. Your home is finally paid for, your kids are all grown up and have their own children, and now it's time to travel and get pleasure from retirement in style. If you are fortunate, you will not have any major health concerns along the way and can spend some of that money you've accumulated.

Finally, as the author of the book of Ecclesiastes so eloquently stated, it is "time to die" (Ecclesiastes 3:2). The cycle ends, and the American dream is over.

But can we be so naïve to believe that just because we live in the United States of America, this so-called dream is what God wants His people to pursue? Does God's Word reveal that followers of Jesus Christ should be controlled by a radically different economic system? Jesus Himself is our main source of instruction on a different economy—one that should govern the life of a Christian. But before we get to that point, let's explore some things the Word of God reveals about real money and sound economics.

## Biblical Currency

From the beginning of history, true wealth has been measured in useful commodities that involve hard work to obtain or cultivate. The relative scarcity of the commodity typically increases its value—as demonstrated, for example, by gold, silver, bronze, copper, livestock, and grains. Note how the wealth of Abraham was measured: "And Abram went up out of Egypt, he, and his wife, and all that he had, and Lot with him, into the south. And Abram was very rich in cattle, in silver, and in gold" (Genesis 13:1–2).

Precious metals were the rarest in this list of commodities, thus, were more valuable. These were useful as building materials and for making a myriad assortment of tools and utensils. Though not as rare, livestock and grains were of worth because they were useful for food and clothing. After the Israelites defeated their enemies in the land of Canaan, note the type of wealth Joshua commanded them to take:

> Return with much riches unto your tents, and with very
> much cattle, with silver, and with gold, and with brass,

and with iron, and with very much raiment: divide the spoil of your enemies with your brethren. (Joshua 22:8)

These commodities were also used in place of coins or paper money as a medium of exchange for goods that were needed. As examples, King Solomon used the Israelites' vast store of silver for this purpose, and King Jotham received tribute from other nations in this form:

And a chariot came up and went out of Egypt for six hundred shekels of silver, and an horse for an hundred and fifty: and so for all the kings of the Hittites, and for the kings of Syria, did they bring them out by their means. (1 Kings 10:29)

He fought also with the king of the Ammonites, and prevailed against them. And the children of Ammon gave him the same year an hundred talents of silver, and ten thousand measures of wheat, and ten thousand of barley. So much did the children of Ammon pay unto him, both the second year, and the third. (2 Chronicles 27:5)

While these wares are universally desirable as forms of trade, one drawback of their use as units of exchange is portability. Indeed, it is not easy to lug around large quantities of gold, silver, and grain, or to guide around and keep track of livestock in order to purchase something. As such, the concept of coins was developed as a more portable, more easily transferred store of value.

Unlike the coins used around the world today, however, the early coins contained actual gold and silver, with the value of gold and silver established by a governing body. This meant the coins had "intrinsic value," a worth that belonged to the coin itself, not a value for which the coin had to be exchanged.

The Roman Empire had an extensive and established coinage system that involved both gold and silver. We are twice told stories of Jesus involving coins of the Roman Empire. In one of the accounts, Jewish legal experts tested Jesus regarding payment of the tribute tax to Caesar, and in another, Jesus instructed Peter to catch a fish in which a coin would be found to pay tax to Caesar for both of them.

The Roman Empire is a good example of what can start out good but end up in ruin. In the beginning, the empire's coins, as noted earlier, contained actual precious metals. But the coins lost their intrinsic value as the precious metal content decreased in somewhat parallel fashion to the decline of Rome. There were many reasons for the drop in precious metal content, but historians generally agree the main reason was that the government ran out of "real" money to pay for war and other state expenditures. It was forced to inflate the supply of money and debase the currency, resulting in an ever-decreasing quantity of precious metals in the coins until they had virtually zero intrinsic value. While this allowed the government to create more "money," that money became less valuable to the recipient because it took more of it to buy the same goods, which resulted in a loss of purchasing power.[1] Inflation ensued as a result of an increase in the money supply and debasement of the currency to fiat status, meaning the currency was backed by nothing but faith in the government to make good on the promise to pay value for the currency. If this sounds all too familiar, it is exactly where the United States of America finds itself today—except that the U.S. has gone exponentially farther down the road to inflation and debasement than the Roman Empire ever dreamed. The best way for an individual to combat an environment of currency debasement, where the United States has slowly but surely devolved, is to invest wisely in what the Scriptures define as real money: items such as gold and silver with intrinsic value and relative scarcity. During the period of greatest currency debasement in history, the prices of these precious metals have hit historic highs.

## God's Economy for the Nation of Israel

The Roman Empire fell into a spiral of debt from which it never recovered. Rather than being definitively conquered by an outside army, it gradually faded into oblivion because it ran out of money. This is what many fear the United States of America will face because of its massive debt, which is held by foreign countries and administered by the private Federal Reserve.

The Lord demonstrated to His chosen people, the nation of Israel, that there was a different way—a better way—to run their economy. The insidious nature of debt and usury would not be allowed to spiral out of control under His system. The Lord explained portions of His economic system in Leviticus chapter 25. First, He introduced the concept of debt forgiveness on the year of Jubilee:

> And thou shalt number seven sabbaths of years unto thee, seven times seven years; and the space of the seven sabbaths of years shall be unto thee forty and nine years.
>
> Then shalt thou cause the trumpet of the jubilee to

sound on the tenth day of the seventh month, in the day of atonement shall ye make the trumpet sound throughout all your land.

And ye shall hallow the fiftieth year, and proclaim liberty throughout all the land unto all the inhabitants thereof: it shall be a jubilee unto you; and ye shall return every man unto his possession, and ye shall return every man unto his family. (Leviticus 25:8–10)

Every fiftieth year was a year of Jubilee, in which each Israelite was to forgive the debt of his fellow neighbor. Specifics of the Jubilee year included:

- No planting of crops
- No gathering of crops
- Returning to the original property they owned
- Forgiving debt
- No oppression

Debt forgiveness is a radical concept to the capitalistic world that is built upon debt. But in addition to the forgiveness of debt, the debtor was to be supported by the creditor: "And if thy brother be waxen poor, and fallen in decay with thee; then thou shalt relieve him: yea, though he be a stranger, or a sojourner; that he may live with thee" (Leviticus 25:35).

Another feature of God's economy for the Israelites was lending without usury, or interest. This is another radical concept when compared to capitalism, under which a rate of interest is almost always attached by bank and is a great source of revenue: "Thou shalt not lend upon usury to thy brother; usury of money,

usury of victuals, usury of any thing that is lent upon usury"
(Deuteronomy 23:19).

While the Israelites were not to charge their neighbors interest, no such limitation was placed on debt offered to those of
foreign nations:

> Unto a stranger thou mayest lend upon usury; but unto
> thy brother thou shalt not lend upon usury: that the
> LORD thy God may bless thee in all that thou settest
> thine hand to in the land whither thou goest to possess it.
> (Deuteronomy 23:20)

While the Israelites initially followed these rules, as with other
parts of the covenant God made with them, they abandoned
what He commanded. In the story of Nehemiah rebuilding the
ruins in Jerusalem, there was an outcry by Nehemiah because
the Jewish leaders were not following God's commands regarding
responsible lending to their fellow Jews. The people were being
forced not only to go into debt to buy food and pay taxes, but
they were obliged to offer their property as collateral and send
their children into slavery.

Nehemiah confronted the leaders, reminding them that what
they were doing was against God's covenant. The leaders agreed
that they were wrong and vowed to return the possessions to the
people and release the collateral.

While these concepts established by the Lord in the covenant
He made with the children of Israel would be beneficial to any
nation that followed them, the fact is that they are not observed
today. Even in the time when Jesus walked the earth, Israel had

been infiltrated by Greek and Roman monetary concepts and the Jews had abandoned God's covenant, so these benefits of God's economy were replaced by greed.

## God's Economy and Wealth Accumulation

Though the original concepts God established in His covenant with Israel are not followed in modern times, we can find plenty of guidance in Scripture regarding God's view of economy and wealth. Jesus Himself, as well as His apostles and prophets, showed us God's mind. Let's explore what Scripture has to tell us about money, possessing wealth, and wealth stewardship.

## Money Cannot Be Your Master

First and foremost in God's economy is understanding that money must not be elevated upon a pedestal of worship. You cannot be a servant of money; money must not be allowed to become your master. Jesus made this clear in Matthew 6:24: "No man can serve two masters: for either he will hate the one, and love the other; or else he will hold to the one, and despise the other. Ye cannot serve God and mammon."

"Mammon" is an Aramaic term meaning "wealth" or "possession." Jesus meant that these things, while necessary to survive, must not be idolized. Love must be reserved for God, not for money. Paul stated this in numerous letters because it is an extremely important concept:

But they that will be rich fall into temptation and a snare, and into many foolish and hurtful lusts, which drown men in destruction and perdition. (1 Timothy 6:9)

For the love of money is the root of all evil: which while some coveted after, they have erred from the faith, and pierced themselves through with many sorrows.
(1 Timothy 6:10)

Let your conversation be without covetousness; and be content with such things as ye have: for he hath said, I will never leave thee, nor forsake thee. (Hebrews 13:5)

Paul's admonition was for the Christian to be free from covetousness, or the love of possessions, instead being content with what the Lord provides. In writing to Timothy, Paul testified that the love of money results in leaving the faith and piercing yourself with sorrow. What an awful fate that would be! How easy it can be to let the love of money, chasing wealth, and accumulating possessions consume our lives as we pursue the American dream and climb the worldly ladder of success. Paul prophesied that this would be the case in the last days. He told Timothy that "men shall be lovers of their own selves, covetous, boasters, proud, blasphemers, disobedient to parents, unthankful, [and] unholy" (2 Timothy 3:2).

A disciple of Jesus Christ, however, must be governed by different passions, fighting the good fight of faith and realizing that the world and all its possessions will pass away—and so much the more if I am correct in my belief that we are living in the last of the last days.

## Possessing Wealth, Though Not a Sin, Cannot Consume You

If the love of money must be eschewed by the disciple of Jesus Christ, then would it not be easier to avoid wealth altogether? Perhaps, and God may call some to live in this manner. But there are many examples of wealthy individuals who were also servants of God, including:

- The women who followed Jesus and supported His ministry, such as Joanna the wife of Cuza (Herod's household manager), Susanna, and many others (Luke 8:3)
- Joseph of Arimathea, a member of the Jewish council who did not consent to the plan to kill Jesus, and whom Matthew described as a "rich man" (Matthew 27:57)
- The early Christians and Barnabas, who owned pieces of land and property (Act 4:32–37)

Perhaps King Solomon is the best example of one who understood how to deal with wealth, although it may have taken him a lifetime to gain that understanding. Solomon was endowed by God with unmatched wisdom when, as a young man destined to be king of Israel, he requested it over riches, but he was also granted unparalleled wealth because he asked for wisdom. Consider Solomon's advice regarding accumulating material possessions:

He that loveth silver shall not be satisfied with silver; nor he that loveth abundance with increase: this is also vanity. (Ecclesiastes 5:10)

There is a sore evil which I have seen under the sun, namely, riches kept for the owners thereof to their hurt. (Ecclesiastes 5:13)

What is Solomon's counsel in this passage? That wealth accumulation will not satisfy a person. The key point is in verse 13, where Solomon points out that wealth amassed and hoarded, rather than dispensed to others, is what does the damage. His father, the psalmist David, also warned about accumulating earthly treasures and not allowing them to become what your heart desires: "Trust not in oppression, and become not vain in robbery: if riches increase, set not your heart upon them" (Psalm 62:10).

I believe this is what James had in mind when he gave a grave warning to those who are rich. Reading this passage will give you the impression that there is no hope for those who are rich:

Go to now, ye rich men, weep and howl for your miseries that shall come upon you. Your riches are corrupted, and your garments are motheaten.

Your gold and silver is cankered; and the rust of them shall be a witness against you, and shall eat your flesh as it were fire. Ye have heaped treasure together for the last days.

Behold, the hire of the labourers who have reaped down your fields, which is of you kept back by fraud, crieth: and the cries of them which have reaped are entered into the ears of the Lord of Sabaoth.

Ye have lived in pleasure on the earth, and been wanton; ye have nourished your hearts, as in a day of slaughter. (James 5:1–5)

Given that we know it is possible to be blessed by God with wealth and still be a believer, James' warning may seem confusing. But notice that his words address a specific group of rich people: those who withhold their wealth from those who deserve it, hoarding it in the last days.

Also consider Jesus' famous declaration after encountering the rich young ruler who was not willing to give up his wealth to follow Jesus:

> And when Jesus saw that he was very sorrowful, he said, How hardly shall they that have riches enter into the kingdom of God! For it is easier for a camel to go through a needle's eye, than for a rich man to enter into the kingdom of God. (Luke 18:24)

Here we have an individual who valued his wealth over a relationship with Jesus, and that is why Jesus said it was difficult for those with riches to enter the kingdom of God. Perhaps Paul stated it best when he acknowledged that God's people can be rich, but must trust God, the provider of the riches, rather than the riches themselves: "Charge them that are rich in this world, that they be not highminded, nor trust in uncertain riches, but in the living God, who giveth us richly all things to enjoy" (1 Timothy 6:17).

The disciple of Jesus Christ must seek first God's kingdom and His righteousness, and must not be so concerned about accumulating wealth that it crowds out a relationship with the Father. This means that whatever abundance with which you are blessed by God, it should be used to bless others. This requires proper stewardship of your abundance based on godly principles.

## Being a Good Steward of Wealth

So what is the answer to wealth accumulation and being a good steward of wealth? I believe there are three key steps a Christian must take to become a good steward of wealth:

1. Acknowledge that 100 percent of what you possess belongs to God.
2. Understand God's commands in the Word regarding stewardship.
3. Be content with whatever God has given you.

The first step toward becoming a faithful administrator of what God has given you, and perhaps the most difficult, is acknowledging that 100 percent of your "stuff" belongs to God, not to you. What you do with that 100 percent reveals whether you are a worthy caretaker of God's riches. Some Christians have been taught and believe that God is only entitled to 10 percent of one's income—a tithe that is to be given to the church you attend or to a deserving missionary. But what if God wants you to give 50 percent of your income? Or 70 percent? Are you to answer, "Sorry God, but you only get 10 percent; the rest is mine"? Absolutely not. Scripture is clear that God is the source of all wealth, and everything we have belongs to Him:

And thou say in thine heart, My power and the might of mine hand hath gotten me this wealth. But thou shalt remember the Lord thy God: for it is he that giveth thee power to get wealth, that he may establish his covenant which he sware unto thy fathers, as it is this day. (Deuteronomy 8:17–18)

God made it clear to the children of Israel that He, not the Israelites themselves, was the source of their wealth. In his first letter to the Corinthian church, Paul declared that the church belongs to Christ and was purchased by Him with a great price:

> And ye are Christ's; and Christ is God's.
> (1 Corinthians 3:23)

> For ye are bought with a price: therefore glorify God in
> your body, and in your spirit, which are God's.
> (1 Corinthians 6:20)

If the follower of Jesus Christ is a purchased possession and belongs to God, who can argue against the notion that everything—100 percent—of what that person owns belongs to God? This may be a radical concept to some, but it should not be. How can we give God the credit for blessing us with wealth and possessions, then turn around and believe that He only owns a tenth of it? Anything less than the entire portion is unacceptable. So, does that mean we must sell all of our possessions immediately and give the proceeds to the church? No—and this is where understanding the direction God provides in His Word regarding stewardship of wealth comes in. Acknowledging that God owns all of you and what you possess does not prescribe that you must liquidate everything you own and be ready to hand it out to whoever is in need. Rather, it means that you are constantly mindful to use what you have—what God owns—for His glory.

After acknowledging that God owns everything you have, the second step is understanding what He wants you to do with what He has given you. This is where godly stewardship comes in. We've already discovered that accumulating wealth is not in God's economy for many reasons. Thus, giving away your abundance to those in need—always depending on the Spirit of God for direction—becomes your focus. Paul keyed in on this concept when he commended the Corinthian church for giving to those in need:

> But by an equality, that now at this time your abundance may be a supply for their want, that their abundance also may be a supply for your want: that there may be equality: As it is written, He that had gathered much had nothing over; and he that had gathered little had no lack. (2 Corinthians 8:14–15)

In quoting from Exodus chapter 16, Paul provides guidance for the Christian regarding having abundance. In the passage from Exodus, the one who ended up with abundant manna in the wilderness was to give to those who gathered less. In this way, the one who had gathered much had no overabundance, and the one who had gathered little had no lack. Paul applied this passage to the Christian life, establishing the concept of making certain those who are in need can count on their fellow Christians to help them. This was also a feature of the early Christian church in Jerusalem:

> Neither was there any among them that lacked: for as many as were possessors of lands or houses sold them, and brought the prices of the things that were sold, And laid them down at the apostles' feet: and distribution was made unto every man according as he had need. (Acts 4:34–35)

Giving to others in need shows our love for them, and Paul said that God loves those who cheerfully give of the abundance of their wealth. Jesus confirmed this concept when He admonished us not to accumulate riches on earth, but to store treasures in heaven:

> Lay not up for yourselves treasures upon earth, where moth and rust doth corrupt, and where thieves break through and steal: But lay up for yourselves treasures in heaven, where neither moth nor rust doth corrupt, and where thieves do not break through nor steal. (Matthew 6:19–20)

But how do we define "abundance" so that we can ask the Lord what He would like for us to do with it? Both Jesus and Paul provided answers in the Word. Jesus told us that the Father knows we all need basic necessities: food, clothing, and shelter:

> And seek not ye what ye shall eat, or what ye shall drink, neither be ye of doubtful mind. For all these things do the nations of the world seek after: and your Father knoweth that ye have need of these things. (Luke 12:29–30)

Paul confirmed that having and enjoying the basic necessities of life is the key to contentment: "And having food and raiment let us be therewith content" (1 Timothy 6:8). So, "abundance" in this context would be defined as God's blessings in your life over and above the basic necessities of food, clothing, and shelter. Now, I realize that there are different definitions of these terms, and that is where the liberty that we have in Christ must be followed. We cannot be legalistic and prescribe a certain level to which every person must adhere in this regard. Each person must be fully convinced after prayerfully considering the Scriptures and seeking God's face. Perhaps He has a specific person or ministry that He would like you to bless with a gift? Perhaps you have an abundance of food or clothing God would like you to give someone in need. The key is to continually acknowledge that what you have belongs to God, and remember the important warning Jesus gave regarding how much "stuff" you are able to accumulate: "Take heed, and beware of covetousness: for a man's life consisteth not in the abundance of the things which he possesseth" (Luke 12:15). To avoid coveteousness, always ask the Lord what He would like for you to do with your abundance.

This leads to the final step in being a good steward of what God has given you: being content with what you have. This may sound easy, but it can be very difficult when your world suddenly falls in on you and you are left with much less than you are used to having. But it is even more difficult, I believe, when you have an overabundance—a true, extra-special blessing of God—and you must acknowledge that it belongs to Him, asking what He would like you to do with it. Being content with what you have sometimes means giving up having more and offering some of that abundance to others. What did Jesus tell us will happen when we give of God's abundance? He said that with the same measure that we give, it will be given back to us:

Give, and it shall be given unto you; good measure, pressed down, and shaken together, and running over,

shall men give into your bosom. For with the same measure that ye mete withal it shall be measured to you again.
(Luke 6:38)

We can truly be content with what we have only when we
are willing to give it all away, if that is what God requires. Most
likely, He will not ask that of us. But we must make God's kingdom our focus and obsession, and if we do, He promises to add
all the things we need to our lives: "But rather seek ye the kingdom of God; and all these things shall be added unto you" (Luke
12:31).

Being content with whatever state you are in becomes much
easier when you realize that you are the precious, purchased possession of Jesus Christ, and that you are not of this world. This
life is but a vapor, and everything in the world will someday be
burned up. Your focus should not be on the riches of this world,
but on promoting God's kingdom, remembering that a much
greater reward awaits us in eternity.

## Summary

God's Word reveals that followers of Jesus Christ should be controlled by a radically different economic system than the one the
world has to offer. God's economy is based on real money—commodities that are scarce and useful—rather than on debt and fiat
currency. Gathering riches on earth and pursuing wealth are to be
eschewed in favor of accumulating treasure in heaven and seeking
the kingdom of God and His righteousness. Giving a portion of

your abundance to others in the body of Christ who are lacking will result in God's lavish blessing in your life.

If there is one thing I'd like for you to take away from this chapter, it would be to remember that 100 percent, not just 10 percent, of your possessions belong to Him. Being faithful with what God has provided will not be a successful venture without this admission.

## chapter two

# MODERN MONEY
*Blind Faith and Bad Credit*

*By Tony Burtovoy II*

IN ORDER TO understand modern money, one should understand a few basic ideas about the history of money, how it came to be, and how some of history's economic authorities have repeatedly set up and abused the currencies of cities and nations. It will become apparent that modern money and economic systems are built from the very beginning with sinful, unfair, and corrupt scams and schemes from top to bottom. Exhaustive detail should not really be needed to comprehend the basics. This chapter will briefly cover some of this history, especially that related to moments when powerful men in charge of historical kingdoms, contrary to the guidance of godly principles found in Scripture, have greedily set up such systems to serve small bands of rich elite at the expense of trusting, uninformed masses.

## Commodity vs. Fiat

Money, simply put, is a standardized means of trading for goods. Historically, many different kinds of commodities have been used as money, but more often, valuable commodities like gold and silver have been used as money. Gold and silver have worked well in ages past because both have rarity and are nearly impossible to manufacture, duplicate, or create. Commodities like grains, animals, lumber, or anything else organic would not serve well as money because they can be duplicated over and over again. Other items like rocks, shells, salts, or glass would not serve well as money either, because they are far too numerous within the elemental and chemical structure of our planet. If rocks were money, then anyone could become rich simply by walking around and picking up rocks! At first glance, this might seem great, but remember that the amount of goods, services, and foodstuffs produced by human civilizations and by the earth itself are not limitless. They are finite. If everyone was a billionaire because rocks were used as money, there would be a terrible imbalance between the money supply in circulation and the goods, services, and foodstuffs available for purchase. If the supply of money is not properly balanced with the availability of goods and services, then prices will quickly spiral out of control. If a loaf of bread cost ten billion rocks, well, it's certainly easy to see how this would become infeasible on many levels.

Over the course of history, mankind has developed other kinds of economic methods and monetary systems. These systems and valueless substitutes have been put in place and used instead of sound, godly principles and commodities of rarity and a non-creatable nature. The practice of creating a valueless substitute for real money to replace valuable commodities like gold or silver is called "fiat." This can be seen in modern times most commonly as paper notes with government backing. The paper notes have no actual value except for the faith and confidence in the backing authority. On the surface, there seems to be no real problem here, but always remember a central biblical theme: the fallibility, or fallen nature, of mankind. Mankind is in a fallen state and is prone to fall into sin and corruption. Mankind in its fallen state is not capable of handling great power and responsibility without becoming corrupt.

Sir John Dalberg-Acton, an English Catholic historian, politician, and writer in the nineteenth century, made the well-known observation that:

> All power tends to corrupt and absolute power corrupts absolutely. Great men are almost always bad men, even when they exercise influence and not authority: still more when you superadd the tendency or certainty of corruption by full authority.[2]

And then, of course, there are the famous words from the first epistle of Paul to Timothy:

> For the love of money is the root of all evil: which while some coveted after, they have erred from the faith, and pierced themselves through with many sorrows. (1 Timothy 6:10)

So how did these and so many other historical figures reach these conclusions about power and money? Experience, for the most part. The problem with money is that when men of power and authority become corrupt and fall into temptation and sin, they commit evil acts by manipulating money in order to become rich. Manipulation of money is the horrible and dangerous truth behind the concept of fiat money. This goes far beyond simply weighting scales unfairly, and is far more subtle and wicked than overly burdensome interest or usury.

It is important to note that no fiat money system in the history of the world has been prevented from falling into total monetary collapse. This does not bode well for all modern fiat money systems, including those in the United States and other first-world economies, especially in light of the economic troubles boiling to the surface of these modern economies in recent years. When men—fallen in spiritual nature—become tempted to create wealth for themselves by manipulating fiat money (accomplished by printing far more paper notes into existence than is economically realistic), a great imbalance is created in economic markets. Too many paper notes circulate from person to person, and people accumulate a lot of paper notes. When people begin accumulating many paper notes, they can buy more goods and services. If there are not enough goods and services to buy, then demand for those goods and services rises. When demand rises, prices rise. When prices rise, spiritually fallen men are tempted to print even more paper notes to maintain or gain "richness." As this wicked cycle continues, people see increases in prices, or "inflation."

From a physical and mathematical standpoint, a deadly cycle has begun. The paper notes soon become so numerous that they cannot be reliably traced. Estimation comes into play, along with further sinful economic practices such as fractional reserve banking, and soon, paper notes that don't even exist are being recorded in ledgers and computers all throughout the system. At this point, money is exchanged only in "theory." As this cycle continues, it gets worse and worse. Money is eventually created to excessive levels by printing more and more paper notes. All the people in the system think they own a certain number of paper notes, but it's all fantasy—most of it consists of records in ledgers and computers in banks and other financial institutions. The "created" money soon becomes far more plentiful than what's actually been printed by the economic authority. At a certain point, the economic authority has to figure out a way to get some of that physical paper back into the system so that the demand for the paper money can be satisfied. Putting more paper into the system only worsens the situation because the "invisible" money never disappears from the computers and ledgers. It only increases. Mathematically, it's only a matter of time before the value of the overall money supply plummets, as each note put in makes all the notes already circulating worth slightly less. This is a simple mathematical exponent graph. When the value of money plummets, the value of goods and services goes up in the inverse. When people can no longer pay for anything, even food to eat, societies collapse.

## Booms, Busts, and the Ponzi Scheme

Let us take a quick look at the definition of a Ponzi scheme from the U.S. Securities and Exchange Commission website (www.sec.gov):

> **What is a Ponzi scheme?** A Ponzi scheme is an investment fraud that involves the payment of purported returns to

existing investors from funds contributed by new investors. Ponzi scheme organizers often solicit new investors by promising to invest funds in opportunities claimed to generate high returns with little or no risk. In many Ponzi schemes, the fraudsters focus on attracting new money to make promised payments to earlier-stage investors and to use for personal expenses, instead of engaging in any legitimate investment activity.

**Why do Ponzi schemes collapse?** With little or no legitimate earnings, the schemes require a consistent flow of money from new investors to continue. Ponzi schemes tend to collapse when it becomes difficult to recruit new investors or when a large number of investors ask to cash out.

**How did Ponzi schemes get their name?** The schemes are named after Charles Ponzi, who duped thousands of New England residents into investing in a postage stamp speculation scheme back in the 1920s. At a time when the annual interest rate for bank accounts was five percent, Ponzi promised investors that he could provide a 50 percent return in just ninety days. Ponzi initially bought a small number of international mail coupons in support of his scheme, but quickly switched to using incoming funds to pay off earlier investors.[3]

The central theme in a Ponzi scheme is to get a few investors together, build up some cash, get some more investors, use their cash to pay off the earlier investors, and then repeat the process.

Word-of-mouth publicity is generated so all the investors bring in friends or dump in more money because the returns are great. This is repeated until so many people are putting huge amounts of money into the scheme that it becomes advantageous for the organizer to crash everything down, take all the investment money, and disappear. No investor money is ever actually invested in anything! It's just continually passed around by the organizer to keep everyone happy for a while until the investment pool builds up and can be stolen. In the early stages of a Ponzi scheme, the money builds slowly, as it's mostly being used to bring in more and more investors and create a favorable reputation for investment returns. Once the momentum builds and large amounts of money are coming in, it becomes ripe for the picking. This is obviously an evil, wicked, and corrupt scam. In the definition above, the word "investors" is used along with the word "organizers" (Ponzi scheme organizers). If you were to replace the word "investors" with "taxpayers" (or "citizens/debtors") and "organizers" with "government" (or "Federal Reserve"), would the definition still hold true?

"The schemes require a consistent flow of money from new investors to continue," it is stated on the SEC website. "Ponzi schemes tend to collapse when it becomes difficult to recruit new investors or when a large number of investors ask to cash out."[4]

This is exactly what happens in a fiat money system during a bust! If the citizens don't continue to add enough debt to their accounts to support the increasingly large demand for cash in the system, the whole thing collapses. Now, the opposite of a bust is obviously a boom. The boom-bust cycle is continuous by design.

Asset prices collapse and a credit crunch arises, where access to financing opportunities are sharply reduced below levels observed during normal times. The unwinding of the bust phase brings a considerably large reduction in investment and fall in consumption, and an economic recession may follow.[5]

When the bust begins, prices rise, demand falls, and fortunes disappear (except for those in the rich, elite classes who protect themselves with inside knowledge and unfair, sinful dealings). As the recessions wear on and prices finally fall to desirable levels, those who've protected their money (stolen?) begin to reinvest in society and programs at the new, lower price levels. A new boom cycle begins. The middle and lower classes continually rise and fall economically with the repeating waves of the boom-and-bust cycle, while the rich insiders make money during the boom, store it for the upcoming bust, then reinvest at the lows. The insiders who control the boom-bust cycle are at a unique advantage to make money during all phases of the sequence while everyone else simply rises and falls with the repeating waves, sometimes making money and sometimes losing money, but in the end, gaining very little.

## Fractional Banking

James Madison said, "History records that the money changers have used every form of abuse, intrigue, deceit, and violent means possible to maintain their control over governments by controlling money and its issuance."[6] Our Founding Fathers were certainly aware of the evil influences that moneylenders and bankers had on societies past. There's ample evidence in the U.S. Constitution that the government was to have direct control over the issuance of money rather than relinquishing this right to a private, secretive company (the Federal Reserve).

To continue the historical story of gold as money and how fractional banking (as currently practiced by the United States Federal Reserve, which is a private, not a federal, company) can be seen, we look further into this external source:

> The goldsmiths were the first bankers in early England, primarily because people left their gold with the goldsmiths for safekeeping. The first paper money [was] "receipts" for the gold deposits. These represented the gold in storage. These were easier to carry around, and safer, thus making paper money more popular....
>
> The goldsmiths realized, after a while, that few people ever came back to trade in their "receipts" for the gold at any one time. It was at this time that goldsmiths realized they could issue more paper than they had gold to back it up, thus leading the way to a cheated system. Then they could loan out more money than they had, and collect interest on it, as well....
>
> This was the beginning of "fractional reserve banking," or loaning out more money than there is in assets on deposit. This way nobody ever noticed their wealth accumulation....

If you're anyone other than a member bank of the Federal Reserve, you will likely be prosecuted and sent to jail for doing this. Fractional reserve banking is one huge Ponzi scheme that allows an increase in the supply of currency available to make loans to purchase investment capital, without increasing the quantity of investment capital or real savings. The quantity of loans will be higher than the actual supply of saved resources available for investment. Investors will assume that the quantity of loans available represents real savings. This misinformation leads investors to misallocate capital, borrowing and investing too much in long-term projects for which there is insufficient demand and real savings. As investors spend borrowed currency, segments of the economy will boom. Later investors will find the prices of their outputs falling and their costs rising, leading to the failure of new projects and a bust.[7]

Note the use of the term "Ponzi scheme" here! This is incredible. In conclusion, it appears that the boom-bust cycle of most modern fiat money systems is directly created by a scheme put in place to control the money systems of those countries. Spiritually fallen men have succumbed to temptation to enrich themselves at the expense of billions of people. They purposefully manipulate money and support systems that allow them to continue to manipulate and steal everything they can get their hands on. They use the concept of fiat to replace real, "unmanipulatable," money. They manipulate by overprinting, and they introduce sinful rules that seem perfectly logical on the surface, but that behind the scenes allow them to continue to steal the people of the world blind. Since most people of the world are uninterested in such subtle crime, the wicked ones corrupted by great economic power become ever greedier in their crime. "Woe unto them that call evil good, and good evil; that put darkness for light, and light for darkness; that put bitter for sweet, and sweet for bitter!" (Isaiah 5:20).

## Convenient War and Elusive Peace

War is very often associated with economic decline. Major depressions or collapses often spawn war out of necessity. Some might even go so far as to say that wars might be started on purpose in order to resolve a depression or an economic collapse. Of course, this is hard to prove—but it's also hard to refute. History is full of examples of human kingdoms resorting to war in order to escape economic collapse. War is a terrible equalizer. Rules change. Mindsets change. "Groupthink" takes over as people band together for protection, security, and survival. Sacrifices are made. Communication, travel, and speech can be restricted at times. Economics, commerce, and monetary circulation can be suspended, eliminated, or destroyed. Lands and goods trade ownership with victory and loss in battle. When it's all over, fortunes are gone for some (or the people who owned them) and created for others on massive scales. Economies may revalue their currencies, restructure themselves, and/or start rebuilding damage to cities, towns, and lives. It's a very bittersweet way to escape the sinful black hole of economic abuse.

Here is an example from an incident during the later years of the Roman Empire:

A series of civil wars in the third century disrupted society and the empire's trade networks collapsing the economy....

The old Roman Republic experienced years of social strife between classes. By the time the Republic fell into Empire, the elites learned how to deal with the poor. They provided free grain and entertainment in exchange for social peace. By the end of the second century AD, the poor also received free pork. These benefits cost the empire millions, but it could afford the expense until hyperinflation struck in the third century....

In 193, Septimus Severus defeated his rivals in a civil war to claim the imperial throne and found a dynasty. His line devalued the currency in order to enlarge the army and double the legionnaires' pay. Traditionally, emperors kept the military happy since the army often chose Rome's leader. The Severans decided the simplest way to fulfill their obligations was through currency devaluation. Within a century, the Roman denarius was completely worthless.[8]

Interesting. Note that right next to the mentioned "strife" and economic collapse, the article states that the government purposefully devalued the currency in order to create wealth and achieve a desired end, which was to pay off obligations (or debts) and enlarge the army in order to maintain control. War and economic strife here are explicitly connected. Economic strife arises from economic abuse. When the economic system can no longer handle the economic abuse, war becomes ripe for blossom. Many other historical periods also definitively link war to economic collapse as a result of economic abuse of fiat currency. The World War I/World War II period from 1917–1945 was sandwiched around the Weimar Republic collapse in Germany (described in a later chapter) and the Great Depression in the United States. Collapse leads to war, which leads to boom, which leads to bust, which leads to war…it's a deadly cycle. In fact: "Hyperinflation is widely believed to have contributed to the Nazi takeover of Germany and Adolf Hitler's rise to power."[9]

Getting back to the Roman Empire quote above, it does seem that the Roman Empire experienced much of this social strife and civil wars in the later years of its existence. The authorities dealt with this by giving massive quantities of gifts and programs to the poor, most obviously to keep anger from boiling over. When the citizenry is unhappy enough, regimes can be overthrown. Giving gifts might sound like what modern governments do when they overtax middle and upper classes so that the poorer classes can get back big tax returns. And that's not to mention loads of other free programs, including free medicine and healthcare, free food (via food stamps), free money (via unemployment checks), housing assistance, and debt modification. That isn't to say that these freebies are not good ideas in modern societies to help the poor, and it's not to say that people don't sometimes have runs of bad circumstances and need some help. That's not it at all. Rather, it is to say that such programs and freebies certainly would and do keep the poorer classes from rising up in protest more than they might otherwise do if the economic theft of their lives by rich elites were fully exposed.

Make no mistake: Economic abuse by the government is the theft of your life experience. How many miles will you *not* travel because of inflation and prices resulting from economic abuse?

How many vacations will you *not* take? How many long-distance friends will you *not* visit? How many home upgrades will you *not* invest in? How many dollars will you *not* put into your nest egg for retirement? What kind of home, life, or medical care will you have in retirement because you were *not* able to tuck away extra dollars during your younger, more productive years? The richness of your life is transferred from the lower classes, who work and strive for it, to the upper-elite classes, who sit around and dream up schemes to steal your wealth—without your figuring it all out. It's theft of your life and your experiences on this planet, pure and simple. It's almost as if governments take great care to study the masses and have learned over the centuries how to give them just enough to keep them barely viable and breathing—just under the point of meaningful rebellion so that society can continue running while the rich elites remain free to steal the rest of the planet and divide it up among themselves (not to say that they don't fail once in a while). People of all classes who become satisfied with government theft and abuse in exchange for a few freebies and promises of security (that never come true) will never truly have free and full lives. How much more of life could we all have if we just realized such things and peacefully forced governments to obey real laws instead of the ones they pass in the middle of the night or tack onto the fine print of other, unrelated, bills or programs?

Ben Franklin said, "They who can give up essential liberty to obtain a little temporary safety, deserve neither liberty nor safety." He is credited with many other similarly worded truisms, including: "Those who sacrifice liberty for security deserve neither," and "Any society that would give up a little liberty to gain a little security will deserve neither and lose both."[10]

In fact, all of the Founding Fathers of the United States of America were awash in understanding of this concept. Samuel Adams said:

> If ye love wealth greater than liberty, the tranquility of servitude greater than the animating contest for freedom, go home from us in peace. We seek not your counsel, nor your arms. Crouch down and lick the hand that feeds you; May your chains set lightly upon you, and may posterity forget that ye were our countrymen.[11]

Adams and most of the other Founding Fathers understood very well the oppressive and abusive nature of men assigned high authority who had fallen into temptation, sin, and corruption. The U.S. Constitution, the Bill of Rights, and the Declaration of Independence—all penned by men of similar beliefs—expressed parallel ideas, including those expressed by Thomas Jefferson:

> I believe that banking institutions are more dangerous to our liberties than standing armies. Already they have raised up a moneyed aristocracy that has set the government at defiance. The issuing power should be taken from the banks and restored to the people, to whom it properly belongs.... If the American people ever allow private banks to control the issue of currency, first by inflation, then by deflation, the banks and corporations that will grow up around them will deprive the people of all property until their children wake up homeless on the continent their fathers conquered.[12]

So it seems that in his current, fallen state, mankind is incapable of handling the huge responsibility of issuing and controlling money for the good of all without abusing that responsibility and ultimately steering societies into fiat collapse. Now, according to Jefferson's first quote shown above, the "issuing power should be taken from the banks and restored to the people," which is a fantastic first step. However, under the premise that "absolute power corrupts" and "spiritually fallen mankind is doomed to continue in fallibility," one should expect that this hoped-for "transfer" would, given enough time, probably make little difference. Perhaps. But getting the concept into the public domain and out of the secretive and abusive control of a few rich elites behind closed doors—while a great first step—is likely only half the battle. The other half of the battle, in this writer's opinion, would involve doing the following while exercising such authority:

- Seek God's guidance and opinion in all decisions.
- Apply biblical principles and execute them faithfully.
- Trust God's judgment wholeheartedly in all things.
- Get the economic rules and decrees out from behind closed doors for all to see.

No wicked sin produced by minds of evil will be able to withstand the light of public opinion, openness, and godly measurement. Even if we don't currently understand how this might work, can people of faith say that God would not show us how if we stood up and sought Him in all levels of our lives? On a national level, what interesting possibilities come to mind!

*$ $ $*

Ever since the Fall of mankind in the Garden of Eden, people have been in a spiritually fallen state, vulnerable to temptation, sin, and death. Jesus Christ resolved this situation at the cross, but only for those who would willingly accept His blood sacrifice as payment for our eternal lives. Accepting this requires only faith on the part of the believer so that no one may boast about his or her own works having any part in the achievement. Evidence of the conversion is represented in repentance and a changed attitude, which leads to godly works and a full life according to God's will for each of us. Those who reject the will of God in their lives in favor of their own subject themselves to the full measure of repercussions of the fallen nature: temptation, wickedness, and death. Those in rebellion to God's grace compete, betray, and deal wickedly without remorse—and often achieve great authority within business structures, political structures, economic structures, or other influential organizations. When a man or a woman achieves a position of great authority without God in his or her life, that individual becomes the driver of a vehicle of destruction that will harm great masses. People without God in their lives cannot wisely handle great authority, kingship, leadership, or responsibility. All are prone to fall into temptation and sin. When armies and economies are members of the vehicle, then temptation to use those members for theft of wealth and power become too great for mere godless men to resist. Economies become fiat. Fiat becomes abusive. Civilizations become unstable. Economies collapse. War ensues. Wealth is transferred from lower classes to higher classes. And then the deadly cycle begins again. Certainly, no human—believer or unbeliever alike—is destined to fail or succeed based on any single external factor, including religion. However, if those in leadership would faithfully seek God, apply godly principles, and construct economic systems with openness, fairness, and godliness, then the oppression of the boom-bust-war cycle could be lessened or even avoided altogether. At the very least, faithfully seeking God with all our hearts *will* prompt Him to lead us out of our current, errant thinking so we will understand the ways that work and how to use them for good instead of evil. God will not fail us if we choose to act, because God is not a promise-breaker. See for yourself what Holy Scripture has to say on this subject:

**2 Chronicles 7:14:** "If my people, which are called by my name, shall humble themselves, and pray, and seek my face, and turn from their wicked ways; then will I hear from heaven, and will forgive their sin, and will heal their land."

**Ezra 8:22:** "The hand of our God is upon all them for good that seek him; but his power and his wrath is against all them that forsake him."

**Psalms 10:4:** "The wicked, through the pride of his countenance, will not seek after God: God is not in all his thoughts."

**Psalms 32:8–10:** "I will instruct thee and teach thee in the way which thou shalt go: I will guide thee with mine eye. Be ye not as the horse, or as the mule, which have no understanding: whose mouth must be held in with bit and bridle, lest they come near unto thee. Many sorrows shall be to the wicked: but he that trusteth in the LORD, mercy shall compass him about."

**Psalms 34:8–10:** "O taste and see that the LORD is good: blessed is the man that trusteth in him. O fear the LORD, ye his saints: for there is no want to them that fear him. The young lions do lack, and suffer hunger: but they that seek the LORD shall not want any good thing."

**Proverbs 28:5:** "Evil men understand not judgment: but they that seek the LORD understand all things."

**Isaiah 55:6–7:** "Seek ye the LORD while he may be found, call ye upon him while he is near: Let the wicked forsake his way, and the unrighteous man his thoughts: and let him return unto the LORD, and he will have mercy upon him; and to our God, for he will abundantly pardon."

**Hosea 6:3:** "Then shall we know, if we follow on to know the LORD: his going forth is prepared as the morning; and he shall come unto us as the rain, as the latter and former rain unto the earth."

**Hosea 10:12:** "Sow to yourselves in righteousness, reap in mercy; break up your fallow ground: for it is time to seek the LORD, till he come and rain righteousness upon you."

**2 Timothy 3:16–17:** "All scripture is given by inspiration of God, and is profitable for doctrine, for reproof, for correction, for instruction in righteousness: That the man of God may be perfect, thoroughly furnished unto all good works."

## chapter three

# BANKING

## *A Beast Is Brought to Life*

*By Charles W. Gaines*

> "I sincerely believe that banking establishments are more dangerous than standing armies, and that the principle of spending money to be paid by posterity, under the name of funding, is but swindling futurity on a large scale."
>
> —THOMAS JEFFERSON

THE PURPOSE OF this chapter is to inform the reader of the origins of banking, its role and function in modern-day society, and its possible future. This chapter will also present information about the delicate financial condition in which many banks currently find themselves and what steps one can take to minimize the uncertainty that presently exists in the world of banking.

As said in *The Wizard of Oz*, "It is always best to start at the beginning, and all you do is follow the yellow brick road." So it is with understanding modern banking. We, too, will follow a yellow brick road, which in this case is one paved with gold—for the banks, that is. The main title of this book is *Demonomics*, and there is little doubt that Satan, acting through his emissary, the Antichrist, will continue to use today's banking system to help implement the power he wields during the seven-year Tribulation period. The thought of Satan using such a system seems uniquely appropriate, given that banking most likely began in ancient Babylon in the third millennium. Babylon is prominently mentioned in Revelation 17:5 and is referred to as "Mystery Babylon." Isn't it interesting that part of the "mystery" could be the very financial system that was first brought to life there?

Ancient Babylon is well known for its idolatry, and is a general representation of man's rebellion against God in the Holy Scriptures. The central figure of Babylon in its earliest years is Nimrod, who rebelled against God and is often considered to be an Antichrist type. Genesis 10:9 states that Nimrod was a mighty hunter before the Lord. This phrase does not mean that Nimrod was a really good hunter, which pleased the Lord. To the contrary, the words are believed to mean that Nimrod was a warrior or tyrant who pushed his own designs in brazen defiance of his Creator.

The Lord God wanted man to multiply and replenish the earth; that is, He wanted the human race to spread out and inhabit all parts of the earth. Nimrod, however, had other plans. Though Genesis 11 does not specifically mention his name, the statements made in Genesis 10 indicate that Nimrod was "mighty," a literal translation that means he was a chief or king and therefore the one who most likely organized and headed the movement and rebellion mentioned in Genesis 11. It was through Nimrod's direction that a new edict went out—not one intended to multiply and replenish the earth, as the Lord God had directed, but one meant to bring people together in a single place for the purpose of building a tower to preserve their name. Perhaps this was man's first attempt at a one-world order. Thus, through Nimrod's direction, people came together in a single place, pooled their resources and manpower, and proceeded to build the tower of Babel to make a name for themselves (Genesis 11:4). Clearly, in contradiction to God's command, Nimrod's ambition—coupled with an inordinate desire for fame—was to establish an empire by keeping mankind together under his own leadership, lest they be scattered.

Nimrod's plan of building the Tower of Babel failed due to God's intervention, but only in part. This early effort to rebel against God lingered and served as the foundation upon which a banking system would ultimately be built. It would evolve to become a tool by which the rich and powerful, driven by greed, would accumulate vast sums of wealth by transferring it from the masses to themselves through the insidious mechanisms of interest, foreclosure, inflation/currency devaluation, and boom-and-bust economic cycles. In short, it would become a beast with an insatiable appetite.

Make no mistake: It is wealth and money, not governments, that control the world. History has repeatedly shown that governments are easily controlled by those who have the wealth. As Mayer Amschel Rothschild of the famous banking dynasty once said, "Give me control of a nation's money, and I care not who makes the laws." This is a very brazen, but unfortunately true, statement. Controlling wealth is indeed a key tool in manipulating world events. Satan already uses this tool to enslave and ruin lives, and there is little doubt that he will continue to use this system for the same purpose, as Revelation 13:17 teaches.[13] Though banking systems do provide positive benefits to society, such as capitalization and money flow for economic expansion, those benefits come with a very high price tag. Greed, one of Satan's principal tools, is all too often the primary driver behind the more insidious aspects of banking. The character Gordon Gekko, in the movie *Wall Street* directed by Oliver Stone, stated: "The point is, ladies and gentlemen, that greed, for lack of a better word, is good." In man's world, this might be seen as true by some, but greed stands against the principles of God. Webster's defines greed as "a selfish and excessive desire for more of something (such as money) than is needed." God's economy is based on gold and silver as money, trusting for His provision in the lives of believers, and the forgiveness of debt, such as those that occur on the year of Jubilee (see, generally, Leviticus 25). In contrast, man's economy is based on fiat paper money that has no tangible worth, and greed—even at the expense of or harm to others. Additionally, the human economy rests on the premise of encouraging the accumulation of debt by nations and individuals, because debt enslaves. Those who hold the economic keys can then use debt as a means of either controlling those who are indebted or can legally take their property to satisfy the debt.

## The History

The concept of banks began in temples, which later included palaces, and probably predated the invention of money. It was logical that such structures could serve as places in which to store wealth because temples—and similarly, palaces—were the safest locations to store gold, as they were constantly attended and well built. Deposits initially consisted of grain and, later, other goods, including cattle, agricultural implements, and eventually precious metals such as gold. Moreover, there are existing records of loans from the second century BC in Babylon that were made by temple priests/monks to merchants.[14]

Although the general perception may be that organized banking is a relatively new phenomenon that has only developed over the last few centuries, in reality it has existed in one form or another for almost 3,750 years.[15]

It was during the glory days of the Babylonian Empire, from 1728–1686 BC, that the Code of Hammurabi was devised and written. Details of the country's laws and financial regulations were carved on tablets of stone, including the particulars of how loans, interest, and guarantees would operate according to a set of standardized procedures. Thus, the Code of Hammurabi established some important principles, namely that organized banking cannot exist without rules of regulation, political stability, and a developed economy.[16] With the establishment of these principles, the beast was formally brought to life.

The concept of banking did not end with the fall of the Babylonian empire, however. The Romans developed their own domestic banking system based on the use of a universal currency and credit notes. With the expansion of the Roman Empire, countries' borders were crossed, travel throughout the known world became more commonplace, and a need for international banking arose, which the Roman government accommodated.[17]

By way of the Romans' robust banking system, foreigners could trade with confidence throughout the Roman Empire, knowing that definite rules applied. So, it was the Romans who crucially introduced legislation to regulate financial institutions and practices.[18]

During the thirteenth century, Italy became a center for moneylenders to the rich and powerful rulers of Europe, including the papacy. It was through the Italians that the double-entry (i.e., credit/debit entries) form of bookkeeping and bill of exchange (the forerunner of today's check) were introduced. Additionally, the famous gold coin known as the "florin," which came to be highly recognized and trusted, was also introduced.[19] The florin was the hard currency of its day—money in the truest sense, and a far cry from the fiat currencies that flood today's financial institutions.

However, one particularly troubling pattern was also established during this time, and that was the concept of banks loaning vast sums of money to rulers of countries, such as Edward III of England, to finance wars and other governmental endeavors, thereby creating the first national deficits held by privately owned banks. This theme was to reoccur through the centuries to the present day.

During the sixteenth century, the beast continued to evolve and became even more sophisticated when the concept of fractional banking was invented. Fractional banking came about when the banks realized that only a portion of the deposits were ever demanded by their depositors at the same time. With this recognition, they developed the idea of fractional banking and began loaning out for interest the part of their deposits that were not in demand by depositors. In short, banks could make money with their depositors' money by lending it out with little risk of all of the deposits being required at the same time. This idea of fractional banking has survived to the present day and has become even more commonly implemented and abused by banks.

The seventeenth and eighteenth centuries found further advancements and sophistication in the banking industry with the advent of national banks, such as the Bank of England, and paper money in Europe.[20] Additionally, along with the colonization of the Americas, the financial beast easily jumped the pond and took root in the new land. The colonies and even the newly formed United States government attempted to control spending, currency devaluation, and inflation by using a hard-money currency, such as silver, for a short time. However, it was not long before they gave in to the seductive lure of printing fiat money.[21] Fiat money has a very simple definition: "paper money decreed to be legal tender, not backed by gold or silver."[22] In essence, *it is money created from absolutely nothing and has no tangible value other than what people or governments are willing to ascribe to it.* Its only backing is "full faith and credit," as the saying goes. It is this simple concept that banks quickly embraced and have continued to use to this present day all over the world.

So, what was started by King Hammurabi of ancient Babylon more than four thousand years ago has grown and evolved into the beast we now refer to as westernized banking. Not only has the beast grown and evolved, it has become firmly established across the globe and its tentacles extend into nearly every aspect of our daily lives.

## Types of U.S. Financial Institutions

The following are the different types of financial institutions in the United States available to consumers: national banks, state banks, savings and loans, and credit unions. At one time, each institution was different in the types of services it performed. Presently, however, the differences between these institutions are much less pronounced, and all currently have some type of insurance for respective depositors.[23, 24, 25] However, they still differ in specialization, emphasis, and regulatory and supervisory structures.

## Central Banks

Yet another type of bank is more preeminent than all other types of banks: the central bank. There are different levels of central banks: international central banks and national central banks.

### *The International Central Bank*

The Bank for International Settlements (BIS) has been called "the central bank of central banks" because it fosters international monetary and financial cooperation and serves as a bank for central banks.[26] Though its primary office is located in Basel, Switzerland, in a building appropriately called the "Tower of Basel" (sound familiar?), it is not accountable to any national government. The BIS carries out its work through subcommittees, the secretariats it hosts, and its annual general meeting of all members, which comprise various central banks from around the world, including the United States. It also provides banking services exclusively to central banks and international organizations like itself.[27]

Interestingly, BIS had a somewhat sinister beginning. It was first formed in 1930 by Montagu Norman, the then-governor of the Bank of England, and his German colleague, Hjalmar Schacht—later Adolf Hitler's finance minister. After World War I, the need for the bank was suggested as a means of transfer for German reparations payments. During the period from

1933–45, the board of directors of the BIS included Walter Funk, a prominent Nazi official, and Emil Puhl. Both were convicted at the Nuremberg trials after World War II. The board also included Herman Schmitz, the director of IG Farben, and Baron von Schroeder, the owner of the J. H. Stein Bank, whose bank held the deposits of the Gestapo. Given its apparent close ties to the Gestapo, there were allegations that the BIS had helped the Germans loot assets from occupied countries during World War II,[28] the purest form of wealth transfer.

Recently, one author observed:

> The trend towards some sort of global governance is best represented by the efforts of bank supervisors under the aegis of the Bank for International Settlements in Basel to impose common minimum capital requirements on banks...and to integrate and coordinate the supervision of banking, securities markets and insurance.[29]

In contemplating this statement, little imagination is needed to see that such a bank, having powers of international scope and whose members and ownership reside in a handful of national central banks, could easily be used by the Antichrist to gain economic control of the world's economy with the mark of the Beast being the fiat currency of that day.

### National Central Banks

A national central bank issues currency, regulates money supply, and controls interest rates in a country. Central banks also oversee the commercial banking system within its country's borders. A central bank is distinguished from a normal commercial bank in that it has a monopoly on creating the currency of that nation, which is usually that nation's legal tender.[30,31] The primary function of a central bank is to provide the nation's money supply, but more active duties include controlling interest rates and acting as a lender of last resort to the banking sector during times of financial crisis. It may also have supervisory powers to ensure that banks and other financial institutions do not behave recklessly or fraudulently.[32] Most economically developed nations today have an "independent" central bank, that is, one that operates under rules designed to prevent political interference.

The Federal Reserve Bank is the central bank of the United States and consists of twelve regional Federal Reserve member banks, with boards of directors, under an umbrella direction of the seven-member Federal Reserve Board in Washington. The directors have the power to determine major aspects of banking activity, such as setting interest rates, the reserve amount member banks are required to keep with them, and other operational requirements. Purportedly, there are no shares of the Washington Federal Reserve Board organization; the only "ownership" of the Federal Reserve is in shares of each of the twelve regional banks, which are entirely owned by the private member banks within their respective districts. The ownership is further determined according to a formula based on size. The ownership is highly restricted in that such ownership is mandatory, the shares can't be sold, and they pay a guaranteed 6 percent annual dividend.[33]

The titles and functions of these central banks lead most people to believe that they are institutions of their respective governments. However, this is an aspect of central banks that is hotly disputed. For example, there are those who suspect that a primary owner of the Federal Reserve is the famous Rothschild family, along with a select few wealthy American families and the large banks that they control.[34] This suspicion arises from the fact that Paul Warburg, allegedly a representative of the Rothschild family, and an elite handful of American families were instrumental in forming the Federal Reserve and the legislation necessary to give it its monopolistic and expansive powers.[35] The Federal Reserve's official statement on its ownership, however, is that it is not "owned" by anyone and is not a private, profit-making institution. Instead, it is an independent entity within the government, having both public purposes and private aspects.[36]

To the point of profit, the Federal Reserve reported that it paid more than $45 billion of its profits to the United States Treasury in 2009.[37] However, one source notes that the banking profits, coming through the privileged money-creation process, mainly occur at the member-bank level, and those profits, estimated to be between $100–200 billion per year, are not turned over to the U.S. Treasury.[38]

The debate over who owns the Federal Reserve and exactly where its profits go will evidently continue, but one thing is indisputably clear: The Federal Reserve—as is the case with most, if not all, central banks—has the unfettered authority to print as much fiat money as it wants. This gives central banks significant control over economies and money supply, and it is by this mechanism that central banks can create inflation and boom-and-bust economic cycles,[39] which in turn can be used to transfer wealth from the masses to a select few. For example, in the United States, purportedly under 1 percent of the population currently claims ownership to almost 50 percent of the wealth.[40] This is a disturbing statistic, and unfortunately one that most likely will only continue to get worse.

## Feast of the Beast

Now that a basic summary of the origins and history of banking has been presented, a discussion of how modern banks operate and earn money will be undertaken.

The avenues by which banks make money have greatly expanded over the past century. In the beginning, banks made money primarily by lending depositors' money out, charging interest on those loans, and charging customers safekeeping fees. The income garnered from lending (often referred to as "interest income") was not insignificant because through the concept of fractionalized banking, a bank could lend the bulk (up to 90 percent) of its depositors' money without great risk of it being demanded all at once. The application of this principle significantly expanded the profitability of banks.

As banks became more sophisticated over the last century, they ventured into other avenues of "noninterest income" generation, such as fees for various banking transactions, investment banking, securities brokerage, insurance agency and underwriting, mutual funds, and investing in the stock market.[41] Using the various income-generating mechanisms at their disposal, banks effectively transfer wealth from everyday people to themselves. The transfer is quiet and pernicious, and occurs unrecognized by the common masses.[42]

### Interest Income

Many understand how banks derive interest income because we have inevitably been participants, in one way or another during our lives, by borrowing money to purchase a car, a house, or appliances, or by paying interest on a credit card. Using the money of its own depositors or money that it cheaply borrows from the Federal Reserve, a bank loans a supposed credit-worthy borrower money for some intended purchase at a set interest rate. In return, the bank receives interest-and-principal payments from the borrower while obtaining a lien or mortgage in the property or some other tangible asset of the borrower. The act of lending does two things: one, it actually creates money; and two, it creates debt for the borrower.[43]

The amount of interest the borrower is charged varies depending on that person's credit rating, which banks use to help measure the risk of the loan. The lower the credit rating, the more interest the bank charges. Thus, as it turns out, the more economically disadvantaged a person is, the more that he or she ultimately pays for the car, home, or appliance, due to the higher interest rate. The interest rate also depends on the Federal Reserve discount rate or the Federal Reserve funds rate the bank has to pay, which has been historically low since the last quarter of 2008. For example, the Federal Discount Rate, the interest rate at which an eligible financial institution may borrow funds directly from the Federal Reserve Bank, has ranged from historic lows of 0.50 percent to 0.75 percent as of February 10, 2011.[44] The spread between the cost of funds a bank must pay in the form of interest and what it charges borrowers is healthy, particularly where interest on credit cards is concerned.

When money is lent, debt is created. Debt enslaves borrowers and gives control over one's finances to the lender, with foreclosure being the tool that provides the control through fear of foreclosure or repossession. As Christ Jesus said, you cannot serve two masters. It is impossible to serve both man and God (see Luke 16:13). One must wonder what master we serve as a nation when considering the national and private debt of the United States. To that point, when including all of the future obligations associated with governmental programs such as Social Security and Medicare, along with the current national deficits of $14 trillion, the national debt currently stands at approximately $118.8 trillion. Unbelievably, this figure is nearly twice the gross domestic product (GDP) of the entire world[45, 46] and equates to approximately $383,000 per person in the United States. Moreover, if this staggering national debt were not enough, the private debt as of 2008 in the U.S. stood at $14 trillion![47] Obviously, given these numbers, we as a nation are severely enslaved—indeed, even addicted—to debt. It is an addiction born out of a desire to obtain things in a vain attempt to satisfy an emptiness only Christ Jesus can fill, helped along, of course, by the willing hand of a banking system all too eager to lend money.

## Noninterest Income

Over the last century, banks have become progressively more innovative in the way they make a profit, and over the last two decades, banks' noninterest income has risen significantly. As noted above, during the period from 1986 to 2003, though interest income of commercial banks decreased by approximately 17 percent, noninterest income of banks increased by 17.2 percent during that same time.[48] Since 1999, the rise in noninterest income was possible due to deregulation that opened the door for commercial banks to earn fee income from investment banking, merchant banking, insurance agencies, securities brokerage, and other nontraditional financial services. Thus, there was little difference between a regular bank and an investment bank. The key deregulation was the Gramm-Leach-Bliley Act of 1999 that created a financial holding company framework allowing common ownership of and formal affiliation between banking and nonbanking activities.[49]

The amount of profit a large national bank can generate using nontraditional methods can be significant. The banks' (including large investment banks') involvement in the markets has generated a bit of discussion indicating that banks are generating huge profits from trading securities. For example, nearly 75 percent of Goldman Sachs' $13.4 billion profit for 2009 came from trading securities for its own benefit.[50] One must suspect that such a large market marker in securities would have an inside advantage on any trade it makes, thereby giving it an unfair advantage over smaller investors. Further, Bank of America reported second-quarter profits for 2010 in the amount of $2.6 billion from trading bonds, currencies, and commodities, and about $1 billion from stock trading.[51] Given these large profits, it is easy to see that banks can make significant earnings by investing money that doesn't even belong to them, that is temporarily loaned to them by the U.S. government, or that they can borrow very cheaply from the Federal Reserve.

## The Wealth Transfer

Banks use different types of mechanisms to transfer wealth, cycling the economy from boom to bust or creating inflation/currency devaluation by printing fiat currency.

## Boom to Bust

One way in which wealth is often transferred is through boom-and-bust economic cycles. Using the power of the money-printing press, the Federal Reserve pumps money into a particular sector of the economy. This classically overheats or inflates the targeted sector, which in turn causes a crash, making properties or assets cheap. The banks, including the Federal Reserve, can then purchase those assets at substantially reduced values and sell them when the market turns around. The turnaround in the markets can often be the result of a change in the Federal Reserve's economic and monetary policies.

The most recent example of a boom-to-bust cycle is the housing bubble of 2007. It began early in 2000, when the Federal Reserve decided to pump money into the housing market. The Federal Reserve did this by lowering interest rates to encourage people to purchase homes. As such, the program involved supplying money to the housing industry for the purpose of lending money at low rates to borrowers who, in most cases, were not financially able to afford the homes. However, the banks seemed somewhat cavalier about the lending process because the reigning, but now defunct, presumption at the time was that housing prices would continue to rise for some indefinite period. If default occurred, the bank would receive the property back under foreclosure and easily resell it for a profit. Thus, all of the interest—plus any increase in equity or profit the borrower might have had in the house—would inure to the benefit of the bank. In other words, wealth would be transferred from the borrower to the bank; in short, the bank wins, the borrower loses.

Things rocked along nicely under this scenario from about

2000 to 2007. Interest rates, courtesy of the Federal Reserve, were at historic lows, housing prices seemed as though they would always go up, and banks would gladly lend money to the borrowers based on the ever-increasing equity in the house. The borrowers would then spend that money on things such as cars, boats, vacations, and second homes. The economy boomed, and the sky seemed to be the limit. Then something happened; certain astute bankers such as Goldman Sachs began to realize that the housing market was in a bubble after years of being pumped up by the Federal Reserve's cheap interest rates, and it was a matter of time before things came crashing down.

In an effort to reduce risk, banks began packaging all types of mortgages, both good and bad, into an instrument called mortgage-backed securities (MBS), a type of "derivative." Even though the quality of an MBS was actually dubious, credit rating agencies slapped an A+ or better credit rating on them, and the banks began selling those packages to other investment banks or hedge funds, which gladly purchased them based on the housing boom. However, these MBS instruments were so convoluted that the purchasers did not really know what they were buying—and seemed not to care at the time. In addition, those same astute bankers began to take out policies issued by large insurance companies on the mortgage-backed securities for the purpose of insuring against defaults, a practice known in the industry as "default credit swaps."

In 2007, the strain on the system became so great that the housing bubble finally burst. Suddenly, investment banks found that they owned what would become known as "toxic assets," because the actual value was much lower than the purchase value. The insurance companies had to start paying off the insurance policies. This put a strain on financial systems, credit markets seized, and things started to unravel quickly.

Because so many large banks, investment banks, and large insurance companies were in trouble by owning or insuring the toxic MBS assets, the U.S. government, with backing from the Federal Reserve, stepped in with the largest bailout in U.S. history, known as the Troubled Asset Relief Program (TARP). TARP made about $700 billion immediately accessible to the large national banks, investment banks, and government-run mortgage companies such as the Federal Home Loan Mortgage Corp., (FHLMC), known as "Freddie Mac," and the Federal National Mortgage Association (FNMA), commonly known as "Fannie Mae."

These actions did stabilize the economic banking crisis, but in the process, banks collectively received hundreds of billions of dollars that they could lend or invest—which they evidently chose to invest[52]—if Bank of America's and Goldman Sachs' healthy investment incomes, as discussed above, are any indicator. So, what could have been a financial disaster for the banks turned out to be a profit bonanza instead, courtesy of the U.S. government and the Federal Reserve (i.e., the U.S. taxpayer). Meanwhile, millions of people lost their homes, including all of the equity they had paid into them, and Main Street USA was sacrificed to save Wall Street.

## Inflation Equals Devaluation

Another tool used primarily by central banks to transfer wealth is to create inflation by printing excessive amounts of money, which also devalues the currency. Remember, the Federal Reserve has the unfettered right to print as much money as it wants, and it costs the Federal Reserve nothing. Since 1913, the Federal Reserve has done such an excellent job of this that the dollar has lost approximately 96 percent of its value. In 2007, it would have taken $21.60 to buy the same amount of goods as $1 bought in 1913. Moreover, since the end of 2001, the United States dollar has lost 37 percent of its purchasing power when compared to a basket of other countries' currencies, which has caused its status as the world's reserve currency to be seriously questioned. The economic crisis of 2008 also caused the Federal Reserve to unleash hundreds of billions of new dollars into the system in an effort to keep the beast going, and 2010 saw the Federal Reserve implementation of its "quantitative easing" policies to help stimulate the economy. Under this program, the Federal Reserve is buying hundreds of billions of dollars worth of U.S. Treasury notes and bonds—with printed money, of course, because no other investors will purchase them. Always remember, each time the Federal Reserve prints money, the value of your dollar goes down farther.

If this scenario continues, the endgame will result in a dollar that is virtually worthless. Thus, the value you have built over a period of years, if kept in dollars, will have substantially eroded away. When the Roman government devalued its currency to the point of being worthless, the government fell.

## Endgame

Where are banking and the U.S. dollar headed? Most likely, in the U.S., banks will continue to consolidate into ever-larger banks, and many more will be merged or closed as a result of failure. In

1986, there were 3,799 commercial banks, and by 2003, there were 2,662 commercial banks. This decline occurred as a result of small- or medium-sized banks merging with larger, national banks and as a result of a significant number of bank failures.[53] The number of banks continues to decline in light of mergers and bank failures, thereby consolidating banking functions into ever-larger megabanks. Since the financial crisis of 2008–2010, approximately 322 banks failed in the United States,[54] and more failures are expected. This is in contrast to only five bank failures in the five years preceding 2008.[55]

Also, as the U.S. dollar becomes more worthless, the nations of the world will press ever harder for a world reserve currency. The world bank, the BIS, is already in place, and the calls for abandoning the U.S. dollar in favor of a world currency are growing in number by the day. The BIS and one-world currency will be equipped and positioned to serve the Antichrist's plans to control the world's economies well.

What does this mean for Christians, and what practical steps, if any, can be taken? First and foremost, "Trust in the LORD with all thine heart, and lean not unto thine own understanding. In all thy ways acknowledge him, and he shall direct thy paths" (Proverbs 3:5–6). Remember, it all belongs to Him, and you are the steward of the things He has entrusted to you. Trust in Him only, and in no tangible thing or system. Second, through prayer, seek God's guidance in these matters. Everyone's financial situation is different; therefore, no one solution addresses all circumstances.

However, there are some basic, common-sense steps that one may take, given the financial situation we currently face. Store up some extra food and water in the house. Buy a freezer and fill it.

Keep extra canned goods and dry goods above that which you ordinarily keep. Given the amount of inflation that we can expect in view of continued currency printing and devaluation, it is only logical to believe that massive inflation is just around the corner. So, food most likely is as cheap as it will be for the foreseeable future.

Keep debt to a minimum and try to eliminate it completely, if possible. Also, if you are in a position to do so, it might be wise to purchase gold or silver bullion (coins). These metals have historically represented true money throughout the centuries, so in a period when paper currencies are becoming less valuable by the day, gold and silver may not be a bad form of money to possess. But be careful! Seek out a reputable gold dealer and avoid gold coin scams, which are occurring with greater frequency.

Also, check up on your bank's financial health rating. One place you can go is: www.thestreet.com, where you can access Weiss' Ratings for banks. For example, according to Weiss Research, a total of 2,667 U.S. banks and thrifts now merit a rating of D+ or lower.[56]

## Conclusions

1. Today's banking system, which includes powerful central world and national banks, is used to transfer wealth.
2. Wealth transfer can be accomplished through debt creation.
3. Wealth transfer can be accomplished through inflation/currency devaluation and the ability to endlessly print money.

4. Banks will continue to consolidate in preparation for the arrival of the one-world government and the Antichrist.
5. Know the strength of your bank.
6. Purchase extra food items and gold or silver, if possible.
7. The Lord God is sovereign and in control, so trust in Him completely and in no device or system of man.

## chapter four

# THE FEDERAL RESERVE SYSTEM

## The Creature from Jekyll Island

*by G. Edward Griffin*

WHAT IS THE Federal Reserve System? The answer may surprise you. It is not federal, and there are no reserves. Furthermore, the Federal Reserve Banks are not even banks. The key to this riddle is found not at the beginning of the story, but in the middle. It is not a curriculum to be mastered, but a mystery to be solved. So let us start where the action is.

## The Journey to Jekyll Island

The basic plan for the Federal Reserve System was drafted at a secret meeting held in November of 1910 at the private resort of J. P. Morgan on Jekyll Island, off the coast of Georgia. Those who attended represented the great financial institutions of Wall Street and, indirectly, Europe as well. The reason for secrecy was simple. Had it been known that rival factions of the banking community had joined together, the public would have been alerted to the possibility that the bankers were plotting an agreement in restraint of trade—which, of course, is exactly what they were doing.

What emerged was a cartel agreement with five objectives: stop the growing competition from the nation's newer banks; obtain a franchise to create money out of nothing for the purpose of lending; get control of the reserves of all banks so that the more reckless ones would not be exposed to currency drains and bank runs; get the taxpayer to pick up the cartel's inevitable losses; and convince Congress that the purpose was to protect the public. It was realized that the bankers would have to become partners with the politicians and that the structure of the cartel would have to be a central bank. The record shows that the Fed has failed to achieve its stated objectives. That is because those were never its true goals. As a banking cartel, and in terms of the five objectives stated above, it has been an unqualified success.

## The Structure and Function of the Federal Reserve System

The three main components of the Fed are: (1) the national Board of Governors, (2) the regional Reserve Banks, and (3) the Federal Open Market Committee. Lesser components include: (4) the commercial banks, which hold the stock, and (5) the advisory councils.

The national Board of Governors determines the system's monetary policy and consists of seven members who are appointed by the president and confirmed by the Senate. The chairman of the board controls the staff and is the single most powerful influence within the system.

The regional Reserve Banks hold cash reserves of the system, supply currency to member banks, clear checks, and act as fiscal agent for the government. The twelve regional Reserve Banks are located in Atlanta, Boston, Chicago, Cleveland, Dallas, Kansas City, Minneapolis, New York, Philadelphia, Richmond, San Francisco, and St. Louis.

The federal government does not own any stock in the system. Banks hold the stock, but each bank is entitled to only one vote, regardless of the amount of stock it holds. In reality, the stock is not evidence of "ownership," but simply represents how much operating capital each bank has put into the system. It is neither a government agency nor a private corporation in the normal sense of the word. It is subject to political control; yet, because of its tremendous power over politicians and the elective process, it has managed to remain independent of political oversight. Simply stated, it is a cartel, and its organizational structure is uniquely structured to serve that end.

The Federal Open Market Committee implements the monetary policy set by the national board, although it exercises considerable autonomy in setting its own policy. It manipulates the money supply and interest rates primarily by purchasing or selling government securities—although it also accomplishes that through the purchase or sale of foreign currencies and the securities of other governments as well. Money is created and interest rates go down when it purchases. Money is extinguished and interest rates go up when it sells. Policy is formulated on a daily basis. In fact, it is monitored by the minute, and the committee often intervenes in the market to effect immediate changes.

All Fed decisions are made at secret meetings. A brief report is released to the public six weeks later, but transcripts of the deliberations are destroyed. That policy was begun in 1970 when the Freedom of Information Act was passed. Not even the CIA enjoys such secrecy.

## The Name of the Game Is Bailout

Although national monetary events may appear mysterious and chaotic, they are governed by well-established rules that bankers and politicians rigidly follow. Central to understanding these events is that all the money in the banking system has been created out of nothing through the process of making loans. A defaulted loan, therefore, costs the bank little of tangible value, but it shows up on the ledger as a reduction in assets without a corresponding reduction in liabilities. If the bad loans exceed the size of the assets, the bank becomes technically insolvent and must close its doors. The first rule of survival, therefore, is to avoid writing off large, bad loans, and—if possible—to at least continue receiving interest payments on them. To accomplish that, the endangered loans are rolled over and increased in size. This provides the borrower with money to continue paying interest, plus fresh funds for new spending. The basic problem is not solved, but it is postponed for a little while and made worse.

The final solution on behalf of the banking cartel is to have the federal government guarantee payment of the loan should the borrower default in the future. This is accomplished by convincing Congress that not to do so would result in great damage to the economy and hardship for the people. From that point forward, the burden of the loan is removed from the bank's ledger and transferred to the taxpayer. Should this effort fail and the bank be forced into insolvency, the last resort is to use the Federal Deposit Insurance Corp. (FDIC) to pay off the depositors. The FDIC is not insurance, because the presence of "moral hazard" makes the thing it supposedly protects against more likely to happen. Some FDIC funds are derived from assessments against the banks. Ultimately, however, they are paid by the depositors themselves. When these funds run out, the balance is provided by the Federal Reserve System in the form of freshly created new money. This floods through the economy, causing the appearance of rising prices but in reality lowering the value of the dollar. The final cost of the bailout, therefore, is passed to the public in the form of a hidden tax called inflation.

## Protectors of the Public

The game called "bailout" is not a whimsical figment of the imagination; it is real. Here are some of the big games of the past and their final scores.

In 1970, Penn Central Railroad became bankrupt. The banks that loaned money to it had taken over its board of directors and put it farther into the hole, all the while extending bigger loans to cover the losses. Directors concealed reality from stockholders and made additional loans so the company could pay dividends to keep up a false front. Directors and their banks unloaded their stock at unrealistically high prices. When the truth became public, stockholders were left holding the empty bag. The bailout involved government subsidies to other banks to grant additional loans. When Congress was told that the collapse of Penn Central would be devastating to the public interest, it responded by granting $125 million in loan guarantees so banks would not be at risk. The railroad failed anyway, but the banks were covered. Penn Central was nationalized into Amtrak and continues to operate at a loss.

In 1970, as Lockheed Corp., a major U.S. aircraft manufacturer, faced bankruptcy, Congress heard essentially the same story. Thousands would be unemployed, contractors would go out of business, and the public would suffer greatly. So Congress guaranteed $250 million in new loans, which put the corporation 60 percent deeper into debt than before. Now that the government was guaranteeing the loans, it made sure Lockheed became profitable by granting lucrative defense contracts at noncompetitive bids. The banks were paid back.

In 1972, the Commonwealth Bank of Detroit, with $1.5 billion in assets, became insolvent. It had borrowed heavily from Chase Manhattan to invest in high-risk and potentially high-profit ventures. Now that it was in trouble, so was Chase. The bankers went to Washington and told the FDIC the public must be protected from the great financial hardship that would follow if Commonwealth folded. So the FDIC pumped in a $60-million loan, plus federal guarantees of repayment. Chase took a minor write-down but converted most of its potential loss into taxpayer-backed assets.

In 1975, New York City had reached the end of its credit rope. It had borrowed heavily to maintain an extravagant bureaucracy and a mini welfare state. When Congress was told the public would be jeopardized if city services were curtailed and that America would be disgraced in the eyes of the world, it authorized $2.3 billion in additional loans, which more than doubled the size of the current debt. The banks continued to receive their interest.

In 1978, Chrysler was on the verge of bankruptcy. Congress was told that the public would suffer if the company folded, and that it would be a blow to the American way if freedom of choice was reduced from three to two makes of automobiles. So Congress guaranteed up to $1.5 billion in new loans. The banks reduced part of their loans and exchanged another portion for preferred stock. The banks' previously uncollectible debt was converted into a taxpayer-backed, interest-bearing asset.

In 1979, the First Pennsylvania Bank of Philadelphia became insolvent. With assets in excess of $9 billion, it was six times the size of Commonwealth. It, too, had been an aggressive player in the seventies. Now the bankers and the Federal Reserve told the FDIC that the public must be protected from the calamity of a bank failure of this size, and that the national economy—perhaps even the economy of the entire world— was at stake. So the FDIC gave a $325 million loan—interest-free for the first year, and at half the market rate thereafter. The Fed offered money to other banks at a subsidized rate for the purpose of relending to First Penn. With that enticement, they advanced $175 million in immediate loans, plus a $1 billion line of credit.

In 1982, Chicago's Continental Illinois became insolvent. It was the nation's seventh-largest bank, with $42 billion in assets. The previous year, its profits had soared as a result of loans to high-risk business ventures and foreign governments. Although it had been the darling of market analysts, it quickly unraveled when its cash flow turned negative. Fed Chairman Paul Volcker told the FDIC it would be unthinkable to allow the world economy to be ruined by a bank failure of this magnitude. So, the FDIC assumed $4.5 billion in bad loans and took 80 percent ownership of the bank in the form of stock. In effect, the bank was nationalized—but no one called it that.

Bailouts up to this point pale in comparison to the trillions of dollars pumped into banks, insurance companies, automobile manufacturers, and banks of other countries beginning in 2008. It started with what was called the subprime meltdown, caused by a calculated policy of the nation's largest banks to entice low-income families into accepting mortgages in excess of what they could afford. The assumption was that the value of houses would rise forever, so people could pay off old loans by taking out larger, new loans based on the increasing value of real estate. These doomed mortgages were packaged together, given fancy names, and sold to naive investors and investment funds. When the day of reckoning arrived, millions of mortgage holders lost their mythical equity (and their homes) while millions of investors lost their money.

The banks that created this bubble were on the brink of collapse, but carefully following the rules of the game, they told Congress they were too big to fail, because if they did, so would America itself. Congress dutifully approved virtually every request for taxpayer funding, regardless of the amount. This legalized plunder was coordinated by two secretaries of the Treasury, Henry Paulson and Timothy Geithner, who came from the banking fraternity and used their positions of public trust to protect and enrich the cartel.

All of the money was provided by the Federal Reserve acting as the "lender of last resort." That was one of the purposes for which it had been designed. We must not forget that the phrase "lender of last resort" means that the money is created out of nothing, resulting in the confiscation of wealth through inflation.

## Home Sweet Loan

Our present-day problems within the savings-and-loan industry can be traced back to the Great Depression of the 1930s.
Americans were becoming impressed by the theories of socialism
and soon embraced the concept that it was proper for government to provide benefits for its citizens and protect them against
economic hardship.

Under the Hoover and Roosevelt administrations, new government agencies were established that purported to protect
deposits in the S&Ls and subsidize home mortgages for the
middle class. These measures distorted the laws of supply and
demand, and from that point forward, the housing industry was
moved out of the free market and into the political arena.

Once the pattern of government intervention had been established, there began a long, unbroken series of federal rules and
regulations that were the source of windfall profits for managers, appraiser, brokers, developers, and builders. They also weakened the industry by encouraging unsound business practices and
high-risk investments.

When these ventures failed and the value of real estate began
to drop, many S&Ls became insolvent. The federal insurance
fund was soon depleted, and the government was confronted
with its own promise to bail out these companies but not having
any money to do so.

The response of the regulators was to create accounting gim-
micks whereby insolvent thrifts could be made to appear solvent
and thus continue in business. This postponed the inevitable and
made matters considerably worse. The failed S&Ls continued to

lose billions of dollars each month and added greatly to the ultimate cost of bailout, all of which would eventually have to be paid by the common man out of taxes and inflation. The ultimate cost is estimated at over $1 trillion.

Congress appears to be unable to act and is strangely silent. This is understandable. Many representatives and senators are the beneficiaries of generous donations from the S&Ls. But perhaps the main reason is that Congress itself is the main culprit in this crime. In either case, the politicians would like to talk about something else.

In the larger view, the S&L industry is a cartel within a cartel. The fiasco could never have happened without the cartel called the Federal Reserve System standing by to create the vast amounts of bailout money pledged by Congress.

## The New Alchemy

The ancient alchemists sought in vain to convert lead into gold. Modern alchemists have succeeded in that quest. The lead bullets of war have yielded an endless source of gold for those magicians who create money out of thin air. The startling fact emerges that, without the ability to create fiat money, most modern wars simply would not have occurred. As long as this is allowed to function, future wars are inevitable. This is the story of how that came to pass.

### The Rothschild Formula

By the end of the eighteenth century, the House of Rothschild had become one of the most successful financial institutions the world has ever known. Its meteoric rise can be attributed to the great industry and shrewdness of the five brothers who established themselves in various capitals of Europe and forged the world's first international financial network. As pioneers in the practice of lending money to governments, they soon learned that this provided unique opportunities to parlay wealth into political power as well. Before long, most of the princes and kings of Europe had come within their influence.

The Rothschilds also had mastered the art of smuggling on a grand scale, often with the tacit approval of the governments whose laws they violated. This was perceived by all parties as an unofficial bonus for providing needed funding to those same governments, particularly in time of war. The fact that different branches of the Rothschild network also might be providing funds for the enemy was pragmatically ignored. Thus, a time-honored practice among financiers was born: profiting from both sides.

The Rothschilds operated a highly efficient intelligence-gathering system that provided them with advance knowledge of important events—knowledge that was invaluable for investment decisions. When an exhausted Rothschild courier delivered the first news of the Battle of Waterloo, Nathan Rothschild was able to deceive the London bond traders into a selling panic, and that allowed him to acquire the dominant holding of England's entire debt at but a tiny fraction of its worth.

A study of these and similar events reveals a personality profile not just of the Rothschilds, but of that special breed of international financiers whose success typically is built upon certain character traits. Those include cold objectivity, immunity to patriotism, and indifference to the human condition. That profile is the basis for proposing a theoretical strategy called the

Rothschild Formula, which motivates such men to propel governments into war for the profits they yield. The Formula most likely has never been consciously phrased as it appears here, but subconscious motivations and personality traits work together to implement it nevertheless. As long as the mechanism of central banking exists, it will be to such men an irresistible temptation to convert debt into perpetual war and war into perpetual debt.

In the following sections, we shall track the distinctive footprint of the Rothschild Formula as it leads up to our own doorstep in the present day.

## Sink the *Lusitania!*

To finance the early stages of World War I, England and France had borrowed heavily from investors in America and had selected the House of Morgan as the sales agent for their bonds. Morgan also acted as their U.S. purchasing agent for war materials, thus profiting from both ends of the cash flow: once when the money was borrowed and again when it was spent. Further profits were derived from production contracts placed with companies within the Morgan orbit. But the war began to go badly for the Allies when Germany's submarines took virtual control of the Atlantic shipping lanes. As England and France moved closer to defeat or a negotiated peace on Germany's terms, it became increasingly difficult to sell their bonds. No bonds meant no purchases, and the Morgan cash flow was threatened. Furthermore, if the previously sold bonds should go into default, as they certainly would in the wake of defeat, the Morgan consortium would suffer gigantic losses.

The only way to save the British Empire, to restore the value of the bonds, and to sustain the Morgan cash flow was for the United States government to provide the money. But, since neutral nations were prohibited by treaty from doing that, America would have to be brought into the war. A secret agreement to that effect was made between British officials and Col. Edward House, with the concurrence of the president. From that point forward, President Woodrow Wilson began to pressure Congress for a declaration of war. This was done at the very time he was campaigning for reelection on the slogan, "He kept us out of war." Meanwhile, Morgan purchased control over major segments of the news media and engineered a nationwide editorial blitz against Germany, calling for war as an act of American patriotism.

Morgan had created an international shipping cartel, including Germany's merchant fleet, which maintained a near monopoly on the high seas. Only the British Cunard Lines remained aloof. The *Lusitania,* owned by Cunard and operated in competition with Morgan's cartel, was built to military specifications and was registered with the British Admiralty as an armed auxiliary cruiser. She carried passengers as a cover to conceal her real mission, which was to bring contraband war materials from the United States. This fact was known to Wilson and others in his administration, but they did nothing to stop it. When the German embassy tried to publish a warning to American passengers, the State Department intervened and prevented newspapers from printing it. When the *Lusitania* left New York harbor on her final voyage, she was virtually a floating ammunition depot.

The British knew that to draw the United States into the war would mean the difference between defeat and victory, and anything that could accomplish that was proper—even the coldly calculated sacrifice of one of her great ships with Englishmen aboard. But the trick was to have *Americans* on board also, in order to create the proper emotional climate in the United States. As the *Lusitania* moved into hostile waters, where a German U-boat was known to be operating, First Lord of the Admiralty Winston Churchill ordered her destroyer protection to abandon her. This, plus the fact that she had been ordered to travel at reduced speed, made her an easy target. After the impact of one well-placed torpedo, a mighty second explosion *from within* ripped her apart, and the ship that many believed could not be sunk gurgled to the bottom of the sea in less than eighteen minutes.

The deed had been done, and it set in motion great waves of revulsion against the Germans. These waves eventually flooded through Washington and swept the United States into war. Within days of the declaration, Congress voted $1 billion in credit for England and France. Of that, $200 million was sent to England immediately and was applied to the Morgan account. The vast quantity of money needed to finance the war was created by the Federal Reserve System, which means it was collected from Americans through that hidden tax called inflation. Within just five years, this tax had taken fully one-half of all they had saved. The infinitely higher cost in American blood was added to the bill.

Thus it was that the separate motives of such diverse personalities as Winston Churchill, J. P. Morgan, Edward House, and Woodrow Wilson all found common cause in bringing America into World War I. Churchill maneuvered for military advantage; Morgan sought the profits of war. House schemed for political power, and Wilson dreamed of a chance to dominate a postwar League of Nations.

## Masquerade in Moscow

The Bolshevik revolution was not a spontaneous uprising of the masses. It was planned, financed, and orchestrated by outsiders. Some of the financing came from Germany, which hoped that internal problems would force Russia out of the war against her. But most of the money and leadership came from financiers in England and the United States. It was a perfect example of the Rothschild Formula in action.

This group centered mainly on a secret society created by Cecil Rhodes, one of the world's wealthiest men at the time. The purpose of that group was nothing less than world dominion and the establishment of a modern feudalist society controlled by the world's central banks. Headquartered in England, the Rhodes' innermost directorate was called the Round Table. In other countries, there were established subordinate structures called Round-Table Groups. The Round-Table Group in the United States became known as the Council on Foreign Relations. The CFR, which was initially dominated by J. P. Morgan and later by the Rockefellers, is the most powerful group in America today. It is even more powerful than the federal government, because almost all of the key positions in government are held by its members. In other words, it *is* the United States government.

Agents of these two groups cooperated closely in prerevolutionary Russia, particularly after the tsar was overthrown. The American contingent in Russia disguised itself as a Red Cross mission allegedly doing humanitarian work. Cashing in on their close friendship with Trotsky and Lenin, they obtained profitable business concessions from the new government, which returned their initial investment many times over.

## The Best Enemy Money Can Buy

The Bolshevik Revolution was a *coup d'état* in which a radical minority captured the Russian government from the moderate revolutionary majority. They accomplished this through deception, organization, discipline, and surprise. The Red Cross Mission of New York financiers threw support to the Bolsheviks and, in return, received economic rewards in the form of rights to Russia's natural resources, plus contracts for construction and supplies. The continued participation in the economic development of Russia and Eastern Europe since that time indicates that this relationship has survived to the present day. These financiers are not pro-communist or pro- anything else. Their motivation is profit and power. They are now working to bring both Russia and the United States into a world government that they expect to control. War and threats of war are tools to prod the masses toward the acceptance of that goal. It is essential, therefore, that the United States and the industrialized nations of the world have credible enemies. As these words are being written, Russia is wearing the mask of peace and cooperation. But we have seen that before. We may yet see a return of the Evil Empire when the timing is right. United States government and megabank funding—first of Russian, and now of Chinese and Middle-East military capabilities—cannot be understood without this insight.

## A Tale of Three Banks

Those who are ignorant of history, it is said, are doomed to repeat its mistakes. It may come as a surprise to learn that the Federal

Reserve System is America's fourth central bank, not its first. We have been through all this before, and each time the result has been the same.

## The Lost Treasure Map

The Constitution prohibits both the states and the federal government from issuing fiat money. This was the deliberate intent of the Founding Fathers, who had bitter experience with fiat money before and especially during the Revolutionary War. In response to the need to have a precisely defined national monetary unit, Congress adopted the Spanish dollar then currently in use and deemed the content of that dollar to be 371.25 grains of pure silver. With the establishment of a federal mint, American silver dollars were issued in accordance with that standard, and gold *Eagles* also were produced, which were then equal in value to ten silver dollars. Most importantly, free coinage was established wherein Americans were able to convert their raw silver and gold into national coins officially certified by the government as to their intrinsic value. The product of these measures was a period of sound money and great economic prosperity, a period that would end only when the next generation of Americans forgot to read their history and returned to the use of paper money and "bills of credit."

The monetary plan laid down by the Founding Fathers was the product of collective genius. Nowhere in history can one find so many men in one legislative body who understood the fraud inherent in fiat money and the hidden-taxation nature of inflation. There was never such an assembly of scholars and statesmen so determined to set a safe course for the nation of their own creation. Literally, they handed us a *treasure map*. All we had to do was follow it to economic security and national prosperity. But, as we shall see in the following sections, that map was discarded when the lessons of history died out with those who had lived it.

## The Creature Comes to America

America had its first central bank even before the Constitution was drafted. It was called the Bank of North America and was chartered by the Continental Congress in 1781. Modeled after the Bank of England, it was authorized to issue more paper promissory notes than it held in deposits. In the beginning, these notes were widely circulated and served as a national currency. Although the bank was essentially a private institution, it was designed for creating money to lend to the federal government, which it did from the start.

The Bank of North America was riddled with fraud, and it quickly fell into political disfavor. Its inflated bank notes eventually were rejected by ordinary citizens and ceased to circulate outside of the bank's home city of Philadelphia. Its charter was allowed to expire, and in 1783 it was converted into a purely commercial bank chartered by the state of Pennsylvania.

The advocates of fiat money did not give up. In 1791, the First Bank of the United States (America's *second* central bank) was created by Congress. The new bank was a replica of the first, including the fraud. Private investors in the bank were among the nation's wealthiest and most influential citizens, including some congressmen and senators. But the largest investment and the most powerful influence in the new bank came from the Rothschilds in Europe.

The bank set about immediately to serve its function of creating money for the government. This led to a massive inflation of the money supply and rising prices. In the first five years, 42 percent of everything people had saved in the form of money was confiscated through the hidden tax called inflation. This was the same phenomenon that had plagued the colonies less than two decades earlier, but instead of being caused by printing-press money, it was now fueled by fractional-reserve bank notes created by a central bank.

As the time for renewal of the bank's charter approached, two groups with opposite intentions became strange political allies against it: the Jeffersonians, who wanted sound money, and the frontier banks, called wildcatters, who wanted unlimited license to steal. On January 24, 1811, the charter was defeated by one vote in the Senate and one in the House. The central bank was gone, but the wildcatters were everywhere.

The War of 1812 was not popular among the American public, and funding would have been impossible through taxes alone. The government chose to fund the war by encouraging wildcat banks to purchase its war debt bonds and convert them into bank notes, which the government then used to purchase war material. Within two years, the nation's money supply had tripled, and so had prices. Once again, the monetary and political scientists had succeeded in fleecing the American public of approximately 66 percent of all the money they held during that period. And that was on *top* of the 42 percent fleecing they got a few years earlier by the Bank of the United States.

## A Den of Vipers

The government had encouraged widespread banking fraud during the War of 1812 as an expedient way to pay its bills, and this had left the nation in monetary chaos. At the end of the war, instead of allowing the fraudulent banks to fall and letting the free market heal the damage, Congress decided to protect the banks, organize the fraud, and perpetuate the losses. It did this by creating the nation's third central bank called the Second Bank of the United States.

The new bank was almost a carbon copy of the previous one. It was authorized to create money for the federal government and regulate state banks. It influenced larger amounts of capital and was better organized across state lines than the old bank. Consequently, its policies had a greater impact on the creation—and extinguishing—of the nation's money supply. For the first time in our history, the effects began to ricochet across the entire country at once instead of being confined to geographical regions. The age of the boom-bust cycle had at last arrived in America.

In 1820, public opinion began to swing back in favor of the sound money principles espoused by the Jeffersonian Republicans. But since the Republican Party had by then abandoned those principles, a new coalition was formed, headed by Martin Van Buren and Andrew Jackson and called the Democrat Party. One of its primary platforms was the abolishment of the bank. After Jackson was elected in 1828, he began in earnest to bring that about.

The head of the bank was a formidable adversary by the name of Nicholas Biddle. Biddle not only possessed great personal abilities, but many members of Congress were indebted to him for business favors. Consequently, the bank had many political friends.

As Jackson's first term of office neared its end, Biddle asked Congress for an early renewal of the bank's charter, hoping that Jackson would not risk controversy in a reelection year. The bill was easily passed, but Jackson accepted the challenge and vetoed the measure. Thus, a battle over the bank's future became the primary presidential campaign issue.

Jackson was reelected by a large margin, and one of his first acts was to remove federal deposits from the bank and place them into private, regional banks. Biddle counterattacked by contracting credit and calling in loans. This was calculated to shrink the money supply and trigger a national panic-depression, which it did. He publicly blamed the downturn on Jackson's removal of deposits.

The plan almost worked. Biddle's political allies succeeded in having Jackson officially censured in the Senate. However, when the truth about Biddle's strategy finally leaked out, it backfired against him. He was called before a special congressional investigative committee to explain his actions, the censure against Jackson was rescinded, and the nation's third central bank passed into oblivion.

## Loaves and Fishes, and Civil War

The Second Bank of the United States was dead, but *banking* was very much alive. Many of the old problems continued, and new ones arrived. The issuance of bank notes had been severely limited, but that was largely offset by the increasing use of checkbook money, which had no limits at all on its issue.

When the Bank of the U.S. slipped into history, the nation was nearing the end of the boom phase of a boom-bust cycle. When the inevitable contraction of the money supply came, politicians began to offer proposals on how to infuse stability into the banking system. None dealt with the real problem, which was fractional-reserve banking itself. They concentrated instead on proposals on how to make it work. All of these proposals were tried, and they failed.

These years are sometimes described as a period of free banking, which is an insult to truth. All that happened was that banks were converted from corporations to private associations—a change in form, not substance. They continued to be burdened by government controls, regulations, supports, and other blocks against the free market.

The economic chaos and conflict of this period was a major cause of the Civil War. Abraham Lincoln made it clear during his public speeches that slavery was *not* the issue. The basic problem was that the North and the South were dependent on each other for trade. The industrialized North sold its products to the South, which sold its cotton to the North. The South had a similar trade with Europe, and that was an annoyance to the North. Europe was selling many products at lower prices, and the North was losing its market share. Northern politicians passed protectionist legislation putting import duties on industrial products. This all but stopped the importation of European goods and forced the South to buy from the North at higher prices. Europe retaliated by curtailing the purchase of American cotton. That hurt the South even more. It was a classic case of legalized plunder, and the South wanted out.

Meanwhile, powerful forces in Europe wanted to see America embroiled in civil war. If she could be split into two hostile countries, there would be less of an obstacle to European expansion on the North American continent. France was eager to capture Mexico and graft it onto a new empire that would include many of the Southern states as well. England, on the other hand, had military forces poised along the Canadian border ready for action. Political agitators, funded and organized from Europe, were active on both sides of the Mason-Dixon Line. The issue of slavery was but a ploy. America had become the target in a ruthless game of world economics and politics.

## Greenbacks and Other Crimes

It is time now to leave this tragic episode and move along. So let us summarize. America's bloodiest and most devastating war was fought not over the issue of freedom versus slavery, but because of dashing economic interests. At the heart of this conflict were questions of legalized plunder, banking monopolies, and even European territorial expansion into Latin America. The boot print of the Rothschild Formula is unmistakable across the graves of American soldiers on both sides.

In the North, neither greenbacks, taxes, nor war bonds was enough to finance the war. So a national banking system was created to convert government bonds into fiat money, and the people lost over half of their monetary assets to the hidden tax of inflation. In the South, printing presses accomplished the same effect, and the monetary loss was total.

The issuance of the Emancipation Proclamation by Lincoln and the naval assistance offered by Tsar Alexander II were largely responsible for keeping England and France from intervening in the war on the side of the Confederacy. Lincoln was assassinated by a member of the Knights of the Golden Circle, a secret society with rumored ties to American politicians and British financiers. Tsar Alexander was assassinated a few years later by a member of the People's Will, a nihilist secret society in Russia with rumored ties to financiers in New York City, specifically, Jacob Schiff and the firm of Kuhn, Loeb & Co.

As for the "Creature" of central banking, there had been some victories and some defeats. The greenbacks had for a while deprived the bankers of their override on a small portion of government debt, but the National Banking Act quickly put a stop to that. Furthermore, by using government bonds as backing for the money supply, it locked the nation into *perpetual* debt. The foundation was firmly in place, but the ultimate structure still needed to be erected. The monetary system was yet to be concentrated into one central-bank mechanism, and the control was yet to be taken away from the politicians and placed into the hands of the bankers themselves. It was time for the Creature to visit Congress.

## The Harvest

Monetary and political scientists continue to expound on the theoretical merits of the Federal Reserve System. It has become a modern act of faith that economic life simply could not go on without it. But the time for theory is past. The Creature moved into its final lair in 1913 and has snorted and thrashed about the landscape ever since. If we wish to know if it is a creature of service or a beast of prey, we merely have to look at what it has done. And, after the test of all those years, we can be sure that what it has done, it will continue to do. Or, to use the biblical axiom, a tree shall be known by the fruit it bears. Let us now examine the harvest.

## The London Connection

After the Civil War, America experienced a series of expansions and contractions of the money supply leading directly to economic booms and busts. This was the result of the creation of fiat money by a banking system that, far from being free and competitive, was a halfway house to central banking. Throughout the chaos, one banking firm, the House of Morgan, was able to prosper out of the failure of others. Morgan had close ties with the financial structure and culture of England and was, in fact, more British than American. Events suggest the possibility that Morgan and Co. was in concealed partnership with the House of Rothschild throughout most of this period.

Benjamin Strong was a Morgan man appointed as the first governor of the Federal Reserve Bank of New York, which rapidly assumed dominance over the system. Strong immediately entered a close alliance with Montagu Norman, governor of the Bank of England, to save the English economy from depression. This was accomplished by deliberately creating inflation in the U.S., which caused an outflow of gold, a loss of foreign markets, unemployment, and speculation in the stock market—all of which were factors that propelled America into the crash of 1929 and the Great Depression of the thirties.

It must be remembered that the same forces were responsible for American involvement in both world wars to provide the economic and military resources England needed to survive.

Furthermore, the key players in this action were men who were part of the network of a secret society established by Cecil Rhodes for the expansion of the British Empire.

## Competition Is a Sin

Banking in the period immediately prior to passage of the Federal Reserve Act was subject to a myriad of controls, regulations, subsidies, and privileges at both the federal and state levels. Popular history portrays this time as one of unbridled competition and free banking. However, as stated above, it was instead a halfway house to central banking. Wall Street, though, wanted more government participation. The New York bankers particularly wanted a "lender of last resort" to create unlimited amounts of fiat money for their use in the event that they were exposed to bank runs or currency drains. They also wanted to force all banks to follow the same inadequate reserve policies so that more cautious ones would not draw down the reserves of the others. An additional objective was to limit the growth of new banks in the South and West.

This was a time of growing enchantment with the idea of trusts and cartels. For those who had already made it to the top, competition was considered chaotic and wasteful. Wall Street was snowballing into two major banking groups—the Morgans and the Rockefellers—and even they had largely ceased competing with each other in favor of cooperative financial structures. But to keep these cartel combines from flying apart, a means of discipline was needed to force the participants to abide by the agreements. The federal government was brought in as a partner to serve that function.

To sell the plan to Congress, the cartel reality had to be hidden and the name "central bank" had to be avoided. The word "federal" was chosen to make it sound like it was a government operation; the word "reserve" was chosen to make it appear financially sound; and the word "system" (the first drafts used the word "association") was chosen to conceal the fact that it was a central bank. A structure of twelve regional institutions was conceived as a further ploy to create the illusion of decentralization, but the mechanism was designed from the beginning to operate as a central bank closely modeled after the Bank of England.

The first draft of the Federal Reserve Act was called the "Aldrich Bill" and was cosponsored by Congressman Edward Vreeland, but it was not the work of either of these politicians. It was the brainchild of banker Paul Warburg and was actually written by bankers Frank Vanderlip and Benjamin Strong.

Aldrich's name attached to a banking bill was bad strategy, because he was known as a Wall Street senator. His bill was not politically acceptable and was never released from committee. The groundwork had been done, however, and the time had arrived to change labels and political parties. The measure would now undergo minor cosmetic surgery and reappear under the sponsorship of a politician whose name would be associated in the public mind with anti-Wall Street sentiments.

## The Creature Swallows Congress

President William Taft, although a Republican spokesman for big business, refused to champion the Aldrich Bill for a central bank. This marked him for political extinction. The money trust wanted a president who would aggressively promote the bill, and the man selected was Woodrow Wilson, who had already publicly declared his allegiance. Wilson's nomination at the Democratic National Convention was secured by Colonel House, a close associate of Morgan and Warburg. To make sure that Taft did not win his bid for reelection, the money trust encouraged the former Republican president, Teddy Roosevelt, to run on the Progressive ticket. The result, as planned, was that Roosevelt pulled Republican support away from Taft, and Wilson won the election with less than a majority vote. Wilson and Roosevelt campaigned vigorously against the evils of the money trust while all along being dependent upon that same trust for campaign funding.

When Wilson was elected, House literally moved into the White House and became the unseen president of the United States. Under his guidance, the Aldrich Bill was given cosmetic surgery, and it emerged as the Glass-Owen Bill. Although sponsored by Democrats, in all essential features it was still the Jekyll Island plan. Aldrich, Vanderlip, and others identified with Wall Street put on a pretense of opposing the Glass-Owen Bill to convince Congress and the public that big bankers were fearful of it. The final bill was written with many sound features that were included to make it palatable during congressional debate, but that were predesigned to be dropped in later years. To win the support of the Populists under the leadership of William Jennings Bryan, the Jekyll Island team also engineered what appeared to be compromises, but that in actual operation were, as Wilson called them, mere "shadows"—while the "substance" remained. In short, Congress was outflanked, outfoxed, and outclassed by a deceptive but brilliant psycho-political attack. The result is that on December 23, 1913, America once again had a central bank.

## The Great Duck Dinner

Congress had been assured that the Federal Reserve Act would decentralize banking power away from Wall Street. However, within a few years of its inception, the system was controlled by the New York Reserve Bank under the leadership of Benjamin Strong, whose name was synonymous with the Wall Street money trust.

During the nine years before the crash of 1929, the Federal Reserve was responsible for a massive expansion of the money supply. A primary motive for that policy was to assist the government of Great Britain to pay for its socialist programs, which by then had drained its treasury. By devaluing the dollar and depressing interest rates in America, investors would move their money to England, where rates and values were higher. That strategy succeeded in helping Great Britain for a while, but it set in motion the forces that made the stock-market crash inevitable.

The money supply expanded throughout this period, but the trend was interspersed with short spasms of contraction, which were the result of attempts to halt the expansions. Each resolve to use restraint was broken by the higher political agenda of helping the governments of Europe. In the long view, the result of plentiful money and easy credit was a wave of speculation in the stock market and urban real estate that intensified with each passing month.

There is circumstantial evidence that the Bank of England and the Federal Reserve had concluded, at a secret meeting in February of 1929, that a collapse in the market was inevitable and that the best action was to let nature take its course. Immediately after that meeting, the financiers sent advisory warnings to lists of preferred customers—wealthy industrialists, prominent politicians, and high officials in foreign governments—to get out of the stock market. Meanwhile, the American people were being assured that the economy was in sound condition.

On August 9, the Federal Reserve applied the pin to the bubble. It increased the bank-loan rate and began to sell securities in the open market. Both actions have the effect of reducing the money supply. Rates on brokers' loans jumped to 20 percent. On October 29, the stock market collapsed. Thousands of investors were wiped out in a single day. The insiders who had been forewarned had converted their stocks into cash while prices were still high. They now became the buyers. Some of the greatest fortunes in America were made in that fashion.

## Time Travel into the Future

In the previous sections of this chapter, we have traveled through time. We began our journey by stepping into the past. As we crisscrossed the centuries, we observed wars, treachery, profiteering, and political deception. That voyage has brought us to the present. Now we are prepared to ride our time machine into the future. It will be a hair-raising trip, and much of what lies ahead will be unpleasant. But it has not yet come to pass. It is merely the projection of present forces. If we do not like what we see, we still have an opportunity to change those forces. The future will be what we choose to make it.

### Doomsday Mechanisms

The United States government is mired in a $5.8-trillion debt. By 2001, interest payments on that debt were running $360 billion per year. That consumes about 19 percent of all federal revenue and costs the average family more than $5,000 each year. Nothing is purchased by it. It merely pays interest. It represents the government's largest single expense. Interest on the national debt is already consuming more than 36 percent of all the revenue collected from personal income taxes. If the long-term trend continues, there is nothing to prevent it from eventually consuming all of it.

By 1992, more people were working for the government than for manufacturing companies in the private sector. More citizens are receiving government checks than paying income taxes. When it is possible for people to vote on issues involving the transfer of wealth to themselves from others, the ballot box becomes a weapon whereby the majority plunders the minority. That is the point of no return. It is a doomsday mechanism.

Also by 1992, more than half of all federal outlays went for what are called "entitlements." Here is another doomsday mechanism. Entitlements are expenses—such as Social Security and Medicare—that are based on promises of *future* payments. Entitlements represent 52 percent of federal outlays. When this is added to the 14 percent now being spent for interest payments on the national debt, we come to the startling conclusion that two-thirds of all federal expenses are now entirely automatic, and that percentage is growing each month.

The biggest doomsday mechanism of all is the Federal Reserve System. Every cent of our money supply came into being for the purpose of being loaned to someone. Those dollars will disappear when the loans are paid back. If we tried to pay off the national debt, our money supply would be undermined. Under the Federal Reserve System, therefore, Congress would be afraid to eliminate the national debt even if it wanted to.

Political environmentalism has caused millions of acres of timber and agricultural land to be taken out of production. Heavy industry has been chased from our shores by our own government. High taxes, rules beyond reason for safety devices in the workplace, so-called fair-employment practices, and mandatory health insurance are rapidly destroying what is left of the private sector. The result is unemployment and dislocation for millions of American workers. Government moves in to fill the void it creates, and bureaucracy grows by the hour.

Federal taxes now take more than 40 percent of our private incomes. State, county, and local taxes are stacked on top of that. Inflation feeds on what is left. We spend half of each year working for the government. Real wages in America have declined. Young couples with a single income have a lower standard of living than their parents did. The net worth of the average household is falling. The amount of leisure time is shrinking. The percentage of Americans who own their homes is dropping. The age at which a family acquires a first home is rising. The number of families counted among the middle class is falling. The number of people living below the officially defined poverty level is rising. More and more Americans are broke at age sixty-five.

None of this is accidental. It is the fulfillment of a plan by members of the CFR who comprise the hidden government of the United States. Their goal is the deliberate weakening of the industrialized nations as a prerequisite to bringing them into a world government built upon the principles of socialism, with themselves in control.

The origin of many of the stratagems in this plan can be traced to a government-sponsored think-tank study released in

1966 called the *Report from Iron Mountain*. The purpose of the study was to analyze methods by which a government can perpetuate itself in power—ways to control its citizens and prevent them from rebelling. The conclusion of the report was that, in the past, war has been the only reliable means to achieve that goal. Under world government, however, war technically would be impossible. So the main purpose of the study was to explore other methods for controlling populations and keeping them loyal to their leaders. It was concluded that a suitable substitute for war would require a new enemy that posed a frightful threat to survival. Neither the threat nor the enemy had to be real. They merely had to be believable.

Several surrogates for war were considered, but the only one holding real promise was the environmental-pollution model. This was viewed as the most likely to succeed because (1) it could be related to observable conditions such as smog and water pollution—in other words, it would be based partly on fact and, therefore, believable—and (2) predictions could be made showing end-of-earth scenarios just as horrible as atomic warfare. Accuracy in these predictions would not be important. Their purpose would be to frighten, not to inform.

While the *followers* of the current environmental movement are preoccupied with visions of planetary doom, the *leaders* have an entirely different agenda. It is world government.

## A Pessimistic Scenario

A pessimistic scenario of future events includes a banking crisis followed by a government bailout and the eventual nationalization of all banks. The final cost is staggering and is paid with money created by the Federal Reserve. It is passed on to the public in the form of inflation.

Further inflation is caused by the continual expansion of welfare programs, socialized medicine, entitlement programs, and interest on the national debt. The dollar is finally abandoned as the *de facto* currency of the world. Trillions of dollars are sent back to the United States by foreign investors to be converted as quickly as possible into tangible assets. That causes even greater inflation than before. So massive is the inflationary pressure that industry and commerce come to a halt. Barter becomes the means of exchange. America takes her place among the depressed nations of South America, Africa, and Asia—mired together in economic equality.

Politicians seize the opportunity and offer bold reforms. The reforms are more of exactly what created the problem in the first place: expanded governmental power, new regulatory agencies, and more restrictions on freedom. But this time, the programs begin to take on an international flavor. The American dollar is replaced by a new United Nations money, and the Federal Reserve System becomes a branch operation of the International Monetary Fund/World Bank.

Electronic transfers gradually replace cash and checking accounts. This permits UN agencies to monitor the financial activities of every person. A machine-readable ID card is used for that purpose. If an individual is red flagged by any government agency, the card does not clear, and he or she is cut off from all economic transactions and travel. It is the ultimate control.

Increasing violence in the streets from revolutionary movements and ethnic clashes provide an excuse for martial law. The public is happy to see UN soldiers checking ID cards. The police state arrives in the name of public safety.

Eventually all private dwellings are taken over by the government as a result of bailing out the home-mortgage industry. Rental property is also taken, as former landlords are unable to pay property taxes. People are allowed to live in these dwellings at reasonable cost, or at no cost at all. It gradually becomes clear, however, that the government is now the owner of all homes and apartments. People are living in them only at the pleasure of the government. They can be reassigned at any time.

Wages and prices are controlled. Dissidents are placed into work armies. There are no more autos except for the ruling elite. Public transportation is provided for the masses, and those with limited skills live in government housing within walking distance of their assigned jobs. Men have been reduced to the level of serfs who are subservient to their masters. Their condition of life can only be described as high-tech feudalism.

There is no certainty that the future will unfold in exactly that manner, because there are too many variables. For example, if we had assumed that there will *not* be a banking crisis, then our journey would be different. We would not see long lines of depositors, panic-buying in the stores, or closing of the stock market. But we would still witness the same scenes of despair in the more-distant future. We merely would have traveled a different path of events to get there. That is because the forces driving our society into global totalitarianism would not have changed one iota. We still would have the doomsday mechanisms at work. We would have the CFR in control of the power centers of government and the media. We would have an electorate that is unaware of what is being done to them and, therefore, unable to resist. Through environmental and economic treaties and military disarmament to the UN, we would witness the same emergence of a world central bank, a world government, and a world army to enforce its dictates. Inflation and wage/price controls would have progressed more or less the same, driving consumer goods out of existence and men into bondage. Instead of moving toward the new world order in a series of economic spasms, we merely would have traveled a less violent path and arrived at exactly the same destination.

## A Realistic Scenario

We have finally come to the end of this chapter. It was not a chapter on central banking theory. Without a larger view of war, revolution, depression, and fraud, the case against the Federal Reserve System would be weak. Without that long journey, we would be limited to a sterile discussion of interest rates, discount policies, and reserve ratios. That is not where the body is hidden.

This has been a whodunit, and by now you know the answer.

There are seven reasons to abolish the Federal Reserve System:

- It is incapable of accomplishing its stated objectives.
- It is a cartel operating against the public interest.
- It is the supreme instrument of usury.
- It generates our most unfair tax.
- It encourages war.
- It destabilizes the economy.
- It is an instrument of totalitarianism.

The purpose of this chapter has been to begin to demonstrate the accuracy of those assertions.

The Creature has grown large and powerful since its conception on Jekyll Island. It now roams across every continent and compels the masses to serve it, feed it, obey it, and worship it. If it is not slain, it will become our eternal lord and master.

*Can* it be slain? Yes it can.

*How* will it be slain? By piercing it with a million lances of truth.

*Who* will slay it? A million crusaders with determination and courage. The crusade has already begun.

*$ $ $*

For a far deeper journey into the bowels of the Creature, and for more information on how it can be slain, please read *The Creature from Jekyll Island: A Second Look at the Federal Reserve,* by G. Edward Griffin (American Media, 2010), and visit www. freedom-force.org.

chapter five

# THE REVOLVING DOOR

*Between Bankers, Politicians, the Federal Reserve,
Lobbyists, and Ivy-League Academia*

*By Barry J. Dyke*

A LONG, REVOLVING-DOOR relationship exists between the banking industry, politicians, lobbyists and Ivy-League academia. Many are intimately involved in today's financial meltdown—a financial system that is often more concerned about financial elites than the welfare of taxpayers.

The connections are immense. For more than a decade, I have been researching the revolving-door links between bankers, politicians, the Federal Reserve, and lobbyists—documenting much of this in my first book, *The Pirates of Manhattan*, which was released in 2007, ahead of the financial crisis.

The importance of lobbyists' influence was instilled in me by Paul Craig Roberts, assistant Treasury secretary of the United States under former President Ronald Reagan. Paul illuminated a major problem: Congress no longer makes the final regulations laws. Lawmakers delegate their job to regulators, who are strongly influenced by well-financed lobbyists from corporate America.

Lobbyists, political action committees, not-for-profit think tanks, direct contributors to politicians, and those who orchestrate various soft-dollar arrangements exert tremendous power and influence in this country. I will present the facts, and let you make your own conclusions.

This chapter will first present an overview of lobbying. Second, it will cover the interconnected nature of the academic world in banking and finance. Finally, it will document the revolving-door relationships among all of those already mentioned, from financiers and politicians to Wall Street insiders, Ivy League members, and those who run the Federal Reserve.

## Lobbying—A Carousel of Corruption

Democracy has become a game of insiders and complexity. Lobbyists and politicians are at the heart of this complexity. Often, decisions are made that benefit those with special interests more than they help the common good. These kinds of decisions are made behind closed doors in Washington DC, where Gucci-wearing lobbyists and donation-hungry politicians hammer out the details, away from public view.

Roughly 12,500 lobbyists are registered to operate in the nation's capital, working on everything from healthcare to finance. The amount of spending on lobbying—which lets corporate interests purchase the best laws money can buy—has skyrocketed. According to www.opensecrets.org, lobbyists' spending in

1998 totaled $1.44 billion. By 2009, that amount had jumped to $3.49 billion.

Spending on federal elections, another way to influence laws favorable to banking and finance, has shot up as well. The total dollars used on federal elections, according to figures cited in *The Economist* in January 2011, went from $3.1 billion in 2000 to $5.3 billion in 2008. As a comparison, the British population—even adjusting for the difference in size—spends only 7 percent for parliamentary elections, thanks to spending limits.

Big oil, big agriculture, big unions—big *anything*, for that matter—are big political spenders in Washington. But the financial sector is one of the biggest.

It is not a political issue. Large banks and financial firms load the deck—both Republicans and Democrats are huge recipients of lobbying efforts and political contributions. In the ten-year period beginning in 1998, the financial sector spent more than $1.7 billion in federal campaign contributions and another $3.4 billion on lobbyists. Since 2001, eight of the most troubled financial firms spent over $64 million on congressional candidates.

According to the Center for Public Integrity's 2009–2010 annual report, businesses and trade groups hired more than five lobbyists for each member of Congress in an effort to influence financial regulatory reform. More than 850 banks, hedge funds, companies, and other associations hired three thousand lobbyists to work on financial reform, spending $1.3 billion during the 2009 and 2010 legislative sessions. Goldman Sachs, an investment banking and securities firm, alone had forty-one lobbyists working on legislation favorable to its interests.

Elizabeth Warren, Harvard law professor and overseer of TARP (Troubled Asset Relief Program), estimated that the financial sector spent more than $1.4 million a day to lobby for favorable financial legislation after the worst economic crisis since the Great Depression.

## Repeal of the Glass-Steagall Act

Lobbying has given the banking and financial industries numerous bailouts, subsidies, tax breaks, and back stops[57] while putting the financial welfare of millions in jeopardy. One of the greatest storm-trooper lobbying assaults was the 1999 repeal of the Glass-Steagall Act (GSA), when lobbyists helped bankers retract the separation of investment and commercial banking that had protected this country well since 1933. The GSA had prohibited "tying," the practice of "tying together" commercial loans and investment-banking activities. This practice had been rife with conflicts of interest, as New York banks bought public shaky companies with questionable finances—and consumers were left holding the bag.

The repeal of the GSA was the result of more than $100 million worth of lobbying by banks—led by Citigroup. Lobbyists nicknamed the bill the "Citi-Travelers Act," as Citigroup had acquired Travelers Insurance Co. even when it had been illegal to do so. If Citigroup did not ensure the abolishment of the GSA, it would have had to unwind its acquisition of Travelers. In other words, repealing the act legalized what would have otherwise been an illegal merger.

The repeal of the Glass-Steagall Act immediately opened the door for other financial entities to practice tying as well. They loaded the entities up with too much debt, even as the companies approached bankruptcy. As a result of tying and other factors, two major companies—Enron and WorldCom—collapsed. Citigroup was in the middle of both transactions, paying $3 billion in fines and settlements in its role in financing Enron, and $2.65 billion in 2004 to settle lawsuits for its role in selling stocks and bonds for WorldCom. In 2005, Citigroup forked over another $75 million to settle a court case for its exaggerated research concerning the collapse of Global Crossing, which filed bankruptcy in 2002.

## Predatory Lending

Another example of lobbying that makes the interest of bankers superior to the welfare of taxpayers is the enactment of the Bankruptcy Abuse and Consumer Protection Act of 2005. This lets bankers turn into paupers anyone who defaults on credit cards and student loans. This law is significant, as Congress—in an overwhelming 302–126 vote in the House of Representatives and a 74–25 vote in the Senate—decided in favor of the banks' predatory credit practices in two key areas: credit cards and student loans.

Credit cards are a major source of profits for Bank of America, Citigroup, JPMorgan Chase, Wells Fargo, Capital One, American Express, GE Money, Discover, and others. Already one of the most usury forms of revolving debt in America, credit cards are no longer dischargeable in bankruptcy due to the 2005 act. The law also made student-loan borrowers indentured servants to the student loan industry for life, allowing high-interest, non-negotiable loans and garnishment of wages and disallowing discharge of student loans.

Key politicians behind this bill were then President George W. Bush and then Senator Joseph Biden of Delaware. Both politicians received large campaign financing and other monetary support from credit-card giant MBNA, now the Bank of America. George H. W. Bush, George W. Bush's father and also a former president, received lucrative speaking appearances for MBNA.

Biden, now vice president of the United States, was the shepherd for the Bankruptcy Abuse and Consumer Protection Act of 2005 when he was a senator. MBNA was his largest contributor and one of Delaware's largest employers. Biden's son, R. Hunter Biden, was hired by MBNA after he graduated from Yale law school.

The Student Loan Marketing Association (SLMA, more commonly known as Sallie Mae), is—according to federal reports—the second-largest finance and credit company contributor to federal candidates and parties in 2008 after American Express, another credit card company. In 2006, Sallie Mae was the largest contributor; Capital One was second. In 2004, Sallie Mae was the second-largest contributor, surpassed by MBNA. Albert Lord, the chief executive officer who made about a half of a billion dollars while running Sallie Mae, was so wealthy that, according to CNBC television, he spent more than $30 million to build his own golf course. Sallie Mae has made billions, collecting student loans guaranteed by the taxpayer, even when students default.

Sallie Mae will do just about anything to collect a debt. In 2007, documents surfaced that the organization was trying to use the Freedom of Information Act to force colleges to turn over students' personal information. Sallie Mae is not only a student loan lender, but like JPMorgan Chase's NCO Group, it is a collector of debt. For further information, check out "Student Loan Scams Part 1 & 2 Sallie Mae" on www.youtube.com, which broadcasts the 2006 *CBS News* report on the problems of Sallie Mae.

## Lobbying Turns Your 401(k) into a Gambling Casino

Another notable example of the immense power of lobbying is that performed by the giant mutual funds and asset managers to control Americans' savings with target-date mutual funds.

Target-date mutual funds, which are "set-and-forget" hybrid mutual funds, are highly complex mutual funds that, through lobbying, have become the favored default investment for Americans' 401(k) plans.

According to Morningstar mutual fund research company, target-date mutual funds have taken off like wildfire, going from roughly $65 billion in assets in 2005 to about $330 billion by 2010. Target-date funds became the default investment of choice in 2007 through lobbying the U.S. Department of Labor for the Pension Protection Act of 2006.

This lobbying immensely benefited asset management/mutual fund firms such as Fidelity, Vanguard, T. Rowe Price, BlackRock, Goldman Sachs, the Principal Financial Group, JPMorgan Chase, Wells Fargo, and others. As a result of lobbying, retirement funds are steered into these products, guaranteeing trillions of dollars of assets and billions of dollars in revenues.

However, these target-date funds were a disaster for retail investors in 2008, when the stock market began its meltdown.

Asset allocation and glide-path strategies (which hinge on the principle that as a retirement investor approaches the date of retirement, investments theoretically are supposed to go into less volatile instruments) promoted by mutual companies were a worthless defense in the meltdown. Yet, thanks to lobbying, target-date funds (so complex that not one person in a hundred can understand, measure, or have peace of mind about) are now the favored default investment for America's retirement savers.

Target-date funds are a huge nightmare as well as the latest form of financial alchemy to come out of Wall Street. The January 2011 report from the United States Government Accountability Office (GAO), entitled *Defined Contribution Plans, Key Information on Target Date Funds as Default Investments Should Be Provided to Plan Sponsors and Participants*, illuminated the problems with target-date mutual funds. As one noted benefits attorney said, "If these target-date funds had to pass the FDA [Food & Drug Administration] tests, they would never be in the market." Yet through lobbying, target-date funds have become the favored investment for 401(k) plans, which now constitute the chief retirement strategy for 80 percent of Americans.

These new target-date funds, with absolutely no guarantees, were found to have the following problems, according to the GAO:

- There are no standard design features within the target-date funds. These are "free-for-all" investments that can invest (gamble) in anything.
- All investment risk within a target-date mutual fund is shouldered by the employee rather than the employer or the investment company managing the money.

- Target-date funds do not have a long history. They are relatively new financial products with no proven track record.
- Investment returns vary greatly between target-date funds. Some lost as much as 40 percent of their value during 2008, and an average loss was 23 percent.
- Some target-date funds are behaving like hedge funds with swing-for-the-fences investment styles.
- Some invest in volatile assets such as commodities, derivatives, high-yield debt (junk bonds), and real estate.
- Funds surveyed, which *represented 86 percent of the entire market*, employed an active management investment style that could essentially be changed at the whim of the mutual fund company, thus putting retail investors at risk.
- Plan sponsors—the employers—and employees understand little about target-date funds or how they will perform. Employees are confused by target dates, believing they can retire on a suggested target date.
- Employers have no tools with which to measure or compare target-date funds, and they have limited resources to conduct a thorough selection process.

This author's research and comments, which have been filed with the Securities and Exchange Commission (SEC), the Department of Treasury, and U.S. senators such as Herbert Kohl, found regulators including the White House DO NOT embrace these highly complex funds that private employers are steered into. Both the federal government and the Federal Reserve prefer investments that are backed and guaranteed by the U.S. Treasury and fixed annuities backed by major life insurance companies.

Target-date mutual funds—again, with no guarantees—are now the default investment of choice for America's retirement savers because of immense lobbying efforts by the mutual-fund industry trade group, the Investment Company Institute (ICI), and mutual fund companies such as giant Fidelity.

The regulators' solution to the problem of having no guarantees is to disclose that investments are not guaranteed, that loss of money is possible on or after the target date, and that there is no guarantee that the investment will provide adequate retirement income.

These are just three examples of lobbying. There are many others. Next, let us look at the Harvard and the Ivy League connection to banking, politics, and other people of power in finance.

## The Ivy League Rushes to Wall Street

Harvard, like other elite, eastern, Ivy-League schools, was founded as a divinity school with the primary purpose of educating theologians and ministers so they could help people get closer to God. Now it seems that the primary purpose of Harvard MBA graduates is to make money on Wall Street.

A Harvard MBA costs $112,000—an expensive but lucrative admission pass to the halls of banking, Wall Street, and leveraged buyout finance—not to mention a part of a future government regulator.

According to a November 16, 2010, article by *Yahoo Finance* writer Daniel Gross, "Harvard MBAs are rushing to Wall Street again," and according to MBA data from Harvard Business School, its grads are flocking to Wall Street and banking (see www.hbs.edu/recruiting/mba/resources/career). In the spring of 2008, 41 percent of the graduating class went to "market-sensitive" trades—a fancy name for Wall Street that includes careers in financial services, commercial banking, hedge funds, private equity/leveraged buyouts, and venture capital. In 2009, with markets tumbling, only 28 percent of the graduating class went that route, but as much as 32 percent of the class of 2010 went to Wall Street.

Harvard is not alone in its Ivy-League connection. Graduates of Dartmouth, Yale, Stanford, Columbia, Princeton, and others are all interwoven into the fabric of banking and finance in America—often becoming elite rulers, even when their actual expertise is questionable.

Harvard—which, with the largest financial endowment of any college in the world, should no longer be classified as a not-for-profit divinity school—has been a major player in the speculative investments on Wall Street. Harvard Corp., the endowment management firm for the college, with its swing-for-the-fences endowment, lost $11 billion in 2008.

Harvard was not alone in the speculative access. According to a survey released by the National Association of College and University Business Officers in January 2009 in Washington DC, college endowments lost an average of 23 percent overall. Yale lost about $5.7 billion or 25 percent of its value, Stanford, another endowment with about $17 billion, lost between 20 and 30 percent of its value. Dartmouth lost $700 million, Princeton, with about $16.3 billion, lost about 25 percent, Amherst lost roughly 25 percent of its $1.7 billion endowment, and Columbia lost about the same percentage as Harvard.

The 2010 documentary entitled *Inside Job* did an excellent job of exposing the internal associations between players in banking, the government, and Ivy-League academia. The film—narrated by Matt Damon, produced by Charles Ferguson, and presented with an Academy Award for the best documentary—featured an interview with R. Glenn Hubbard, dean of Columbia Business School. We will reveal his interconnections shortly.

## Revolving Door between Politicians, Banking and the Ivy League

An uncanny, incestuous, chummy connection exists between those involved in banking, Wall Street, the Federal Reserve, the government, politics, and the elite academic world. While not all segments are interlinked, there are clearly overlapping relationships. Consider the following:

**Peter G. Peterson,** former chief executive officer of Lehman Brothers and former secretary of commerce to Richard Nixon, went on to form the Blackstone Group—one of the world's most-powerful, private-equity firms—with Steven Schwarzman (see below). Peterson, with an MBA from the University of Chicago, was the chairman of the Federal Reserve Bank of New York between 2000–2004. When Blackstone went public in 2007, he made $1.8 billion in one day. Schwarzman made $700 million.

**Stephen A. Schwarzman,** cofounder of the Blackstone Group with Peter G. Peterson, graduated from Yale and Harvard Business

School and is one of the wealthiest men in the United States, with a net worth of $4.7 billion (he spent over $3 million for his sixtieth birthday party). Schwarzman, like Peterson, has been taxed at capital-gains rates or "carried interest."

**David Rubinstein,** worth about $2.7 billion, is the founder of the $85-billion, Washington DC, private-equity firm, The Carlyle Group, and was a former deputy policy advisor under the Carter administration. He received a law degree from the University of Chicago.

**George H. W. Bush,** former U.S. president, made appearances for MBNA (formerly Bank of America) and was a special partner to The Carlyle Group. Bush is a Yale alumnus whose family has long-established ties to Wall Street and the oil business.

**Dan Quayle,** former congressman, senator, and vice president of the United States, is an executive with the New York-based private equity firm, Cerberus Capital.

**Arthur Levitt,** a Williams graduate, former banker, and tax-shelter salesman, is past chairman of the SEC and has also been a special partner to The Carlyle Group (2001). He also serves as a policy advisor to Goldman Sachs and as a director of media giant Bloomberg.

**William Kennard,** who graduated from Stanford and Yale law school, is former chairman of the Federal Communications Commission (FCC) and has been a special partner to The Carlyle

Group. He has also been on the board of directors of Hawaiian Telcom, a Carlyle portfolio company that filed bankruptcy in 2008.

**William Jefferson Clinton,** former president of the United States, after leaving the White House, partnered with private-equity baron Ronald Burkle, the supermarket magnate. Burkle helped Clinton make $100 million while at Burkle's Yucaipa Partners, which is funded with hundreds of millions of dollars from the California pension fund CalPERS. The Clinton family also has ties to Los Angeles-based, private-equity financier Haim Saban. Clinton, with a law degree from Yale, made huge fees speaking to investment banks. His wife Hillary, in her run for president, counted Wall Street banks among her major campaign contributors.

**Larry Summers,** former chief economic advisor to President Barack Obama, was an economic advisor under Bill Clinton, former Treasury secretary, and former president of Harvard University. On his watch there, Harvard lost $11 billion of its endowment in overtly aggressive Wall Street bets in hedge funds, private equity, and real estate. Summers earned his undergraduate degree at Massachusetts Institute of Technology and his PhD from Harvard.

**James Rothenberg** is the chairman of Capital Research and Management Co., the mammoth mutual outfit that owns American Funds. Portfolio manager for the Growth Fund of America and Washington Mutual Investors, he was also the treasurer of Harvard when that school lost $11 billion in its endowment and operating accounts. Rothenberg is an alumnus of both Harvard and Harvard Business School.

**Robert Rubin,** Treasury secretary of the United States under Bill Clinton, was previously a key executive at Goldman Sachs. After leaving the Treasury, Rubin held a top position at Citigroup, where he encouraged bankers to take on excessive risk and which ended up being one of the worst-run banks of all time. Rubin, who made more than $100 million at Citigroup, was a 1960 graduate of Harvard. In 2002, he was appointed a member of Harvard Corp., which oversaw the institution's multi-billion-dollar endowment.

**Jeffrey Larson,** former manager for Harvard University foreign stock holdings, made $17.3 million working for Harvard in 2003. He set out to run a hedge fund, Sowood Capital Management, with $350 million in seed money from the university. Sowood collapsed in 2007, losing about $1.5 billion, and was taken over by Kenneth C. Griffin's Citadel.

**Kenneth C. Griffin,** owner of Citadel hedge funds of Chicago, is one of the wealthiest men in the U.S. A Harvard graduate and big supporter of Barack Obama, he started trading in his campus dorm.

**Jack Meyer,** a Harvard Business School graduate, ran the now-infamous Harvard Management Co., which managed the university's endowment. He paid managers tens of millions of dollars, as if they worked on Wall Street. In 2005, he left the company over complaints about pay.

**Robert Glauber,** who served as the interim non-executive chairman of the collapsed Federal Home Loan Mortgage Corp. known as Freddie Mac, lectures at Harvard Business School and has served as the CEO of the National Association of Securities Dealers (NASD). He was also a director of the Investment Company Institute (the powerful, mutual-fund lobbying group), a director at Moody's Corp., a member of the board of the Federal Reserve Bank of Boston, a board member for several Dreyfus mutual funds, and a director of XL Capital. He also served on the Committee for Capital Markets Regulation, the banking group.

**Mohamed el-Erian** was a former International Monetary Fund (IMF) official and manager of the billion-dollar Harvard University endowment, where he received more than $6 million a year. Now the CEO of PIMCO, the bond giant owned by German financial concern Allianz, el-Erian has also served on the faculty at Harvard Business School.

**Kenneth D. Brody,** under Bill Clinton, was president and chairman of the Import-Export Bank and he also worked as head of investment banking and real estate for Goldman Sachs. He is a 1971 graduate of Harvard Business School.

**Timothy Geithner,** Treasury secretary of the United States, was the head of the Federal Reserve Bank of New York, ground zero of the financial meltdown. Geithner also worked for Larry Summers under Bill Clinton's administration, as well as for the International Monetary Fund. Geithner, a Dartmouth graduate, also worked for Henry Kissinger.

**Gary Gensler,** former Goldman Sachs executive, served under Bill Clinton and now heads up the major regulator that forgot to regulate derivatives, the Commodities Future Trading Commission. Gensler received his BS and MBA degrees from Wharton University of Pennsylvania.

**Phil Gramm,** the former Senate banking chairman from Texas, after leaving the Senate, went to work for UBS Warburg—the massive Swiss bank that was bailed out by Swiss taxpayers. Gramm's wife, Wendy, was head of the Commodities Future Trading Commission, which let Enron trade derivatives without regulation. For her work, she became a director of Enron.

**George W. Bush,** former president of the United States, according to www.opensecrets.org, counted among his top campaign contributors from 1989–2008 Morgan Stanley, Merrill Lynch, UBS, Goldman Sachs, MBNA, Credit Suisse, Lehman Brothers, Citigroup, and Bear Stearns. Bush received his MBA from Harvard.

**Jeb Bush,** former governor of Florida and brother to George W. Bush, was a private-equity investment advisor to Lehman Brothers, the largest financial failure in U.S. history.

**R. Glenn Hubbard,** dean of Columbia Business School, holds a PhD in economics from Harvard. He was the chairman of economic advisors under George W. Bush, and was interviewed for the documentary, *Inside Job*, which exposes Hubbard's role in the deregulation of Wall Street while serving under the Bush presidency (which helped ignite the financial crisis). Hubbard has been an economic advisor to Mitt Romney's presidential campaign, he serves as co-chair of the Committee for Capital Markets Regulation, and has been a director for Kohlberg Kravis Roberts, Ripplewood Holdings, and BlackRock.

**Christopher Cox,** former congressman and chairman of the SEC, has an MBA and a doctorate in law from Harvard. When he was thirty-four, he worked for President Reagan. Under Cox's leadership, the SEC proved impotent in ferreting out overleveraged banks and financial frauds from Ponzi schemers Bernard Madoff and R. Allan Stanford.

**David Aufhauser,** one-time senior Treasury official under George W. Bush, received the Alexander Hamilton award, the top recognition for a Treasury official. He was a leading attorney for UBS AG banking giant, and was caught insider trading auction-rate securities, settling with New York Attorney General Andrew Cuomo for $6.5 million. Aufhauser received his MBA from Harvard and a law degree from the University of Pennsylvania.

**John Snow,** former Treasury secretary of the United States, is an executive with the secretive private-equity firm Cerberus Capital, which owned taxpayer-supported Chrysler Motors.

**Robert Zoellick,** on July 1, 2007, was appointed by George W. Bush to be the eleventh president of the World Bank. Also a former managing director at Goldman Sachs (2006–2007), he received his law degree (magna cum laude) and master of public policy at Harvard. Zoellick, a deputy secretary of state under George W. Bush, has been criticized for using his perch in the government for advocating for Wall Street's interest abroad, supporting the privatization of the Japan Post Bank (which began privatization in 2007).

**Steven Friedman,** former chairman of Goldman Sachs as well as an economic advisor to George W. Bush, has served on the board of directors of the Federal Reserve Bank of New York. The Cornell and Columbia graduate received criticism for purchasing $3 million of Goldman Sachs shares while the bank was being supported by the taxpayers.

**Henry Paulson,** former treasury secretary of the United States and a former CEO of Goldman Sachs, is worth more than $500 million—and even owns his own island. He is a Dartmouth grad who also holds an MBA from Harvard (1970).

**Edward Forst,** a former Goldman Sachs banker, worked for the Treasury Department in setting up a bailout fund for the banks. The 1982 Harvard graduate left the Treasury to work for his alma mater as an executive vice president.

**John Edwards,** former senator and presidential candidate, during his time on the campaign trail, spoke of the "fat cats" in Washington while being retained by Fortress Investments, a large manager of hedge funds and private equity. The major money manager was registered in Delaware but had hedge-fund operations registered in the Cayman Islands, helping investors dodge U.S. taxes. For his part-time work with that company, Edwards made $479,000 in 2007. Edwards and his wife reported that they had more than $11.2 million invested in Fortress, with a $29.5-million net worth overall. Edwards later tangled in an extramarital affair with aide Rielle Hunter.

**Michael Novogratz,** a Princeton graduate, is a former Goldman Sachs partner and founder of Fortress Investments. He runs the Fortress Drawbridge Global Macro fund, which got hammered in 2008; it had $8 billion, but between investment losses and redemption requests, plummeted to $3 billion, according to Bethany McLean in an April 2009 *Vanity Fair* article about Fortress entitled "Over the Edge."

**Gary Gorton,** a Yale professor retained by AIG for $1 million a year to make sure its bets in derivatives were correct, is known for his academic papers. In fact, Federal Reserve Chairman Ben Bernanke is a fan of Gorton's work. Gorton convinced Joe Cassano's AIG Financial Products division in London that its foray into the credit-default swap business was as "good as gold." He thought AIG had 10 percent exposure to subprime mortgages, when in reality it was 95 percent. This became the largest bailout in U.S. history.

**Jeffrey Peek** is former CEO of the bankrupt CIT Financial, the New York financial firm that went bankrupt after it received a $2.33 billion taxpayer cash infusion. Despite dismal performance, CIT extended Peek's employment contract for another year in September 2009. Prior to working at CIT, Peek—a Princeton and Harvard grad—was a top executive at Merrill Lynch. CIT went hog wild into student loans and subprime mortgages under Peek's watch.

**John Thain,** a graduate of MIT with an MBA from Harvard, is a former Goldman Sachs key executive who went on to run the New York Stock Exchange. After that, he joined Merrill Lynch and became one of highest-paid bankers on Wall Street in 2007. He reportedly spent more than $1 million decorating his office at Merrill Lynch, which was bailed out by Bank of America via taxpayers. He then became the new CEO of CIT financial, making $6 million a year in 2010.

**Andy Hornby,** a Harvard MBA who graduated at the top of his class, was CEO for the British bank HBOS plc, formerly one of the largest banking groups in the United Kingdom. He was forced to resign after nearly bankrupting the company. HBOS was taken over by Lloyds Banking Group, which was bailed out by British taxpayers. Hornby did not walk away empty handed; he received sixty thousand pounds per month in a "consultancy" contract with Lloyds.

**Barack Obama,** president of the United States, received his law degree at Harvard. His largest campaign contributors included his alma mater and major banks.

**Joe Biden** is the vice president of the United States whose largest campaign contributor when he was a senator from Delaware was MBNA bank (now Bank of America), the huge credit card lender. Biden received $214,000 from employees and executives of MBNA. He backed a tough bankruptcy bill in 2005, which was a legislative priority for MBNA. R. Hunter Biden, his son, was hired out of Yale law school as a consultant to MBNA and worked as a lobbyist that represented biotech, hospital, and colleges looking for earmarks from Congress. The older Biden, according to the nonpartisan Taxpayers for Common Sense, backed $85 million in congressional earmarks for seventy-one projects in 2008 alone. He claimed to be one of the least-wealthy members of the Senate, but according to the Center for Responsive Politics, Biden collected $6.5 million from lobbyists, lawyers, and law firms since 1989.

**James Biden and R. Hunter Biden,** the vice president's brother and son, respectively, owned fund-of-fund hedge fund[58] Paradigm Global Investment Advisors, a feeder fund to R. Allan Stanford, the billionaire who operated a Ponzi scheme out of Antigua that sold bogus certificates of deposit. The Bidens' company, known as Paradigm Global Advisors, received $2.7 million in seed money from the Stanford companies to start their hedge fund in 2007.

**Diana Farrell,** former financial analyst at Goldman Sachs, is now deputy director of the National Economic Council under Barack Obama. She is an alumnus of Wesleyan University and Harvard Business School.

**Rahm Emanuel,** chief economic advisor to President Barack Obama, was once a senior advisor to President Bill Clinton and a banker with Wasserstein Perella, where he made $16.2 million for two years of work. Clinton had Emanuel seated on the board of directors for Freddie Mac, which became plagued with scandals and later collapsed. Emanuel is now mayor of Chicago.

**Steven Rattner,** private-equity founder of the New York-based Quadrangle Group, was President Obama's "car czar," overseeing the collapse and rescue of General Motors. Quadrangle, as well as Rattner, personally, have been fined tens of millions of dollars for kickback schemes with New York state pension funds. Rattner has been chairman of the investment committee at Brown University and manages investments for Michael Bloomberg, the mayor of New York City and one of the wealthiest men in the world.

**Michael Froman,** former operations chief of Citigroup Alternative Investments (hedge funds, private equity, and venture capital), left Citigroup in January 2009 with a $4 million exit package to become a senior White House advisor. Froman holds degrees from Princeton, Oxford, and Harvard—where he was a classmate of Barack Obama while earning his law degree.

**Mark Patterson,** a top lobbyist for Goldman Sachs until 2008, is now Secretary of the Treasury Timothy Geithner's chief of staff.

**Karen Gordon Mills,** in April 2009, was sworn in as Barack Obama's administrator for the Small Business Administration (SBA). Obama commented that she would give America's small business "a partner in Washington." Yet, the Harvard-educated heiress to the Tootsie Roll fortune has been a venture capitalist and manager of private-equity firm Solera Capital of New York City, which was founded in 1999. Most of Solera's funds came from public pension funds such as CalPERS for $72 million, whereas CalPERS has only received $102,000 in distributions as of June 30, 2008.

**Mitt Romney,** former governor of Massachusetts and a presidential candidate, made his fortune in the leveraged-buyout business at Bain Capital, which purchases companies with a Mount Everest of debt. Romney received his law degree and MBA from Harvard. Bain Capital has also secured much of its investment money from Harvard.

**Stephen Pagliuca,** a Bain Capital partner and co-owner of the Boston Celtics, is worth hundreds of millions of dollars. In fact, the Harvard MBA is so wealthy that he followed the footsteps of Romney, with a failed attempt at becoming senator of Massachusetts.

**James Coulter,** the billionaire cofounder of Texas Pacific Group, studied law at Harvard and holds a Stanford MBA. Private-equity highlights include Burger King, Petco, J. Crew, Continental Airlines, and a new albatross, the buyout of TXU, Texas' largest utility, for $45 billion.

**Leon Black,** founder Apollo Management and a Dartmouth graduate who also attended Harvard business school, landed his first gig in investment banking at Drexel Burnham Lambert, the bank that refined the high-yield junk bond (the rocket fuel for the private-equity business). Black is reportedly worth $2 billion. Part of Apollo is owned by CalPERS, the pension fund for California state employees.

**J. C. "Christopher" Flowers,** former banker, once worked with Henry Paulson (noted earlier), Stephen Friedman (also noted earlier), and Jon Corzine, a former Goldman Sachs banker who later became a senator, then governor, of New Jersey, at Goldman

Sachs. A Harvard graduate and major private-equity manager, Flowers moonlights as an investment banker. He played a major role as an advisor in Bank of America's acquisition of Merrill Lynch, receiving payment of $10 million for a weekend of work. Flowers turned into a private-equity rock star, earning himself and another banker, Tim Collins of Ripplewood Holdings, $1 billion each on a Japanese bank deal. He paid $53 million for the Harkness mansion in New York City in 2006, then spent another $15 million to renovate the property—one of the most expensive properties in NYC.

**Theodore "Teddy" Forstmann,** cofounder of the New York-based Forstmann Little private-equity, leveraged-buyout shop, played goalie on Yale's hockey team and earned a law degree from Columbia. He made a fortune buying and selling firms such as General Instruments, Gulfstream Aerospace, and Yankee Candle. Forstmann, according to a 2009 article in *Forbes,* is worth more than $1.1 billion. He has been exposed recently for his huge wagers in sports betting—betting against athletes he represents.

**Louis Moore Bacon,** who runs the secretive hedge fund, Moore Capital, is one of the richest and most successful hedge-fund managers, according to *Forbes*, which reported his worth at $1.5 billion. A Middlebury College graduate and Columbia MBA, he is known for his passion for hunting and a fondness for polo. In 2007, Bacon bought the Forbes family's Colorado ranch for a reported $175 million, one of the highest prices ever paid for a residential property in the U.S. Bacon also owns a 435-acre island in Long Island Sound.

**Michael Cline,** a Harvard MBA and former McKinsey & Co. associate, formed Accretive, a private-equity firm that set its sights on becoming the king of the consumer-debt arbitration business, a lucrative but predatory type of finance. Through its funds, Accretive formed a debt-collecting business called Axiant, which ran call centers and helped collect consumer debts awarded to banks and credit card companies awarded via arbitration.

**Ben Bernanke,** chairman of the Federal Reserve Bank, grew up in South Carolina, played alto sax in the school marching band, and graduated from Harvard summa cum laude. He earned his PhD in economics at MIT.

**E. Gerald Corrigan,** managing director for Goldman Sachs, is former CEO of the Federal Reserve Bank of New York, and was CEO and chairman of the Fed from 1985 to 1993.

**Herbert Allison Jr.**, a former Merrill Lynch executive and former CEO of Teachers Insurance and Annuity Association-College Retirement Equities Fund (TIAA-CREF, one of the largest not-for-profit asset managers in the U.S. for colleges, scientific institutions, hospitals, etc.), has served on the advisory board of the Federal Reserve Bank of New York, where he most recently has been overseeing the government's $700 billion bailout program TARP. Allison holds degrees from Yale and Stanford.

**Peter R. Fisher,** senior official of the Federal Reserve Bank of New York until 2001, as well as former Treasury undersecretary, joined BlackRock money management firm in 2004. He became vice chairman of BlackRock in January 2010, when the firm announced the appointment of Kendrick Wilson, another former Goldman Sachs banker and former Treasury official, to a key executive position.

**Roger Ferguson,** Harvard grad and former vice chairman of the Board of Governors of the Federal Reserve System under Alan Greenspan, is chief executive officer and president of TIAA-CREF.

**William Dudley,** the new Federal Reserve Bank of New York CEO, was the chief economist and managing director for Goldman Sachs for a decade until 2007.

**Lee Bollinger,** president of Columbia University, was named deputy chairman of the New York Federal Reserve Bank in July 2009.

**Richard Fuld,** former CEO of Lehman Brothers, which suffered the largest financial bankruptcy of all time, was once on the board of the Federal Reserve Bank of New York and the board of trustees at Middlebury College.

**Jerry Speyer,** a graduate of Columbia, is a co-chief executive officer of Tishman Speyer Properties, one of the largest real estate developers in the world with more than $35 billion in properties, including the Chrysler Building and Rockefeller Center. Speyer, who chaired the Federal Reserve Bank of New York, with co-manager BlackRock, presided over one of the worst real estate flops in history: the $5.4-billion deal of the eleven thousand-unit Stuyvesant Town Peter Cooper Village, which defaulted in January 2010.

**Jamie Dimon**, CEO of JPMorgan Chase, is on the board of directors for the Federal Reserve Bank of New York. With an undergraduate degree from Tufts and an MBA from Harvard Business School, Dimon addressed the Harvard graduating class in 2009.

**Richard Cashin,** CEO of One Equity, the leveraged buyout/private equity arm of JPMorgan Chase, which purchases companies with massive amounts of debt, holds undergraduate and MBA degrees from Harvard.

**Jeffrey Immelt**, CEO of General Electric, which owns GE Capital (one of the largest banks in the world), serves on the board of directors of the Federal Reserve Bank of New York. With an MBA from Harvard, he graduated with JPMorgan's Jamie Dimon in 1982.

**Larry Kudlow,** the television personality on CNBC, which is owned by General Electric, was once a staff economist at the Federal Reserve; he studied politics and economics at Princeton.

**Maurice "Hank" Greenberg,** former CEO of American International Group, has held a seat on the advisory board of the Federal Reserve Bank of New York.

**Richard Parsons,** chairman of Citigroup, former basketball player, and lawyer, worked on the staff of New York Governor Nelson Rockefeller. When Rockefeller became vice president under Gerald Ford, Parsons followed, working directly with Ford. Parsons then returned to New York as a lawyer in 1977, whereupon he took on Happy Rockefeller, the widow of Nelson Rockefeller, as a major client. After eleven years, Rockefeller became CEO of

Dime Savings Bank, a position he was recruited for by former Rockefeller aide Harry Albright. Dime Savings later merged with Anchor Savings, and Parsons made a bundle of money when the bank was demutualized. Upon the recommendation of Laurence Rockefeller, Parsons became a board member of Time Warner, then president of that $165 billion media empire. Parsons is a special partner to Providence Equity Partners, a private-equity firm with major connections to Citigroup.

**Deval Patrick,** governor of Massachusetts, levied a $4-million fine against Ameriquest in 1996 for ripping off minority- and low-income homeowners when he was a top attorney for the United States Justice Department. Patrick made a 180-degree turn, embracing Ameriquest and going on to receive a $360,000 annual salary as a board member there. He is a graduate of Harvard and Harvard Law School.

**Lewis Kaden,** Citigroup vice chairman and lawyer, helped JPMorgan persuade the government to let the bank underwrite securities again, tearing down the Glass-Steagall Act. He graduated from Harvard, as did all four of his children. One of the most powerful men in Citigroup, Kaden oversees the $45 billion the corporation has received from the press, the government, and the taxpayers.

$$$

As you can see, the revolving-door connections between bankers, politicians, the Federal Reserve, lobbyists, and members of the Ivy-League academic community are immense. Amazingly, this is only a partial list of those links. It's important to keep in mind these connections—and others that may exist—when making political and financial decisions in the days ahead. You, your family, and your community are always better off investing in God and yourselves first.

John D. Rockefeller, one of the nation's first multimillionaires, might have offered some of the best counsel when he said, "I suppose if I was to give advice, it would be [to] stay out of Wall Street."

chapter six

# PERSONAL DEBT

*Economic Slavery*

*By Todd Strandberg*

**N**EVER BEFORE IN history has freedom been in such great abundance. Right now, only about 12 million people are regarded as being trapped in slavery—defined as a system under which people are treated as property and are forced to work.[59]

During the time of the Roman Empire, as much as a third of the population lived in some form of enslavement. One could be enslaved because of debt, enslaved as punishment for a crime, enslaved as a prisoner of war, enslaved because of child abandonment, or enslaved by virtue of being born to slaves.

In the twenty-first century, we have come to abhor slavery so much that we fail to realize how accepted it once was. Slavery was such an ordinary part of life in ancient Greece that it was seldom even commented upon. In fact, most villages had a market square devoted explicitly to the business of trading human beings.

The framers of the United States Constitution were the most liberty-minded people of their age, yet many of them owned slaves. When they said "all men are created equal," the statement was only true for white males of European descent.

Slavery was certainly an evil. Here is what nineteenth-century missionary and explorer David Livingstone wrote of the slave trades:

> To overdraw its evils is a simple impossibility.... We passed a slave woman shot or stabbed through the body and lying on the path. [Onlookers] said an Arab who passed early that morning had done it in anger at losing the price he had given for her, because she was unable to walk any longer. We passed a woman tied by the neck to a tree and dead.... We came upon a man dead from starvation.... The strangest disease I have seen in this country seems really to be broken heartedness, and it attacks free men who have been captured and made slaves.[60]

## Peak Freedom

Many factors led to the banning of slavery. The Christian church played a vital role in the abolitionist movement. Dominican priest Bartolomé de las Casas, who was shocked at the treatment of natives in the New World, convinced Spain to become the first European nation to abolish colonial slavery. A number of anti-slavery societies founded by Christian leaders pressured England to ban slavery in its colonies.

The Industrial Revolution also deserves some credit for ending slavery. When a machine can do a task several thousand times faster than a human, there is less need for forced labor. The increase in the number of skilled tradesmen, craftsmen, and technicians created a mobile labor force that wasn't tied to the land.

Mechanization also reduced the need for personal servants. In pre-industrial times, a king or rich landowner would need at least a hundred slaves to maintain the estate. Tasks like cooking, laundry, farming, and cleaning were all labor intensive. You couldn't just go to a store and buy a loaf of bread. The whole process of growing, harvesting, milling, and baking would require large amounts of time. One slave could spend all day just grinding the wheat into flour. The reason some people have the last name "Miller" is because that was once their ancestors' task in life.

Today, a person of wealth has little need for servants. Most wealthy people have no permanent staff. The ones who do typically hire fewer than a dozen. Mass production allows one person to supply the needs of millions of people. Mr. Miller may still be a miller, but thousands of people who share his name are doing other tasks.

For more than two hundred years, the industrial revolution has been fueled by cheap and plentiful natural resources. We are now starting to run out of some of these riches. The supply of oil is the most important resource. Without it, our transportation system would grind to a halt.

You may have heard the term "peak oil." This is the point at which the maximum rate of global oil extraction is reached, after which the rate of production enters a terminal decline. There is an active debate over when we'll reach peak oil. Some say it has already occurred, while others say we still have an untapped supply. No one can argue against the reality that petroleum will soon be depleted by a skyrocketing global demand.

Even metals like copper and silver are starting to become difficult to extract from the earth. New discoveries of copper are still being made, but the supply peaked in 1996. We may completely run out of the metal in twenty-five years. Silver production has been in decline for several years. In fact, for over a decade, we have been consuming the supply of silver faster than miners can remove it from the ground.

What happens when we start to run out of some of these vital resources? We may find that freedom has also been in a peak cycle. I don't think we are going to return to the horse-and-buggy days, but we may face a sharp reduction in our standard of living.

One of the best measures of affluence is how much the average person spends on food. In the third world, the poor typically use 40 percent of their wages to purchase food. In the U.S., we only devote 12 percent of our income to this category of spending. The down cycle of peak production for oil and other commodities could cause a global depression that would force people into a hand-to-mouth existence. People could spend 50 percent or more of their income on food.

It seems unthinkable that man could step backwards in technological progress, but it has happened in the past. During the Dark Ages, many advances that had been achieved by the Roman Empire were lost. The people of the Dark Ages looked with amazement at the structures the Romans had built.

We don't have a workable plan for finding a viable replacement for oil. Solar power and wind power are friendly to the environment, but these sources of energy will never be able to supply more than 10 percent of our energy needs. Nuclear fusion energy is the only option that can produce meaningful amounts of energy, but it may take decades for us to develop this technology.

The rise of desperate times would not be very conducive to freedom. Whenever the economy suffers, liberty is the first thing to become scarce. And when resources become scarce, people seek profit at the expense of others.

The Bible predicts a time when a man's daily wage will equal the price of a loaf of bread. Whoever controls the supply of grain will control the world:

> And when he had opened the third seal, I heard the third beast say, Come and see. And I beheld, and lo a black horse; and he that sat on him had a pair of balances in his hand. And I heard a voice in the midst of the four beasts say, A measure of wheat for a penny, and three measures of barley for a penny; and see thou hurt not the oil and the wine. (Revelation 6:5–6)

## Why Is Money the Root of All Evil?

The Bible boldly declares that the "love of money is the root of all evil" (1 Timothy 6:10). It may seem odd that Scripture would single out money in this way, placing it even "above" sins such as drunkenness, prostitution, and pornography. What makes the love of money a root cause of evil is what allows these other sins to be so rampant: the greed of people seeking to make a fast buck promoting evil.

Prophecy scholar and author David Reagan once said, "Dig

deep enough into a societal evil; dig all the way down to the root of why that evil is so rampant in the world, and you will find the love of money."[61]

Money is all about the desire to gain status. We measure the value of everything by money. We are greedy to increase our status, and we are jealous when someone has more of it than we do.

In the Christian realm, whole denominations are based on the love of money. The leaders of these churches tell their members that God wants them wealthy, and that they should seek after the finer things of life.

These prosperity preachers try to dance around 1 Timothy 6:10 by saying that you can have all the money in the world—just make sure you don't love it more than God. As one preacher said, "God is not anti-money, or anti-wealth, He is anti-money WORSHIP." A simple way to find out the true nature of these preachers is to examine the teaching material they produce. In most cases, their DVDs, CDs, and books will have an exclusive fixation on gaining wealth.[62]

What gives money the potential for so much evil is its ability to enslave people—without the victims even realizing it. For example, the welfare system in our nation has quietly enslaved millions of people. Just as rat poison is 99.99 percent edible, welfare has a sweetness that hides its negative side. Following are two lengthy examples of how money can secretly rob people of their freedom.

## Alcoholism and Native Americans

Alcoholism runs rampant among Native Americans. The problem is so widespread that it should have been declared a national crisis long ago. The suicide rate for Alaskan tribes is four times the national average, and almost 80 percent of all deaths in that race are related to alcohol abuse or alcoholism.

It is very strange how this problem can be so chronic, yet hardly draws any media attention. The extreme disconnect from reality in this example and in the one to follow is what originally inspired the title of this book. I can only point to demonic delusion as the reason a treatable disease is freely allowed to eat away at a population.

There have been some efforts to control alcohol consumption. Pine Ridge Indian Reservation, on the border between South Dakota and Nebraska, has had a ban on alcohol sales since 1932. Despite the prohibition, four out of every five families in that area have an alcoholic family member. During the winter months, when seasonal construction work disappears, the unemployment rate can hit 90 percent. The poverty rate in the county that is home to the tribe is second in the nation. The poorest county is the nearby Cheyenne River Sioux reservation.[63]

I once visited the Winnebago tribe in North Nebraska and found the area to be one of the most depressing places I've ever been. In one community, bars were the only operating businesses, and everyone walked around like zombies.

A common belief is that Native Americans have a genetic or social weakness for alcohol. This belief scenario is very simple: White men came over from Europe, got the Indians drunk on booze, and then stole their land. However, numerous studies have examined the links between alcoholism and race, with no proof found that Native Americans are more susceptible to alcohol addictions than other racial groups. Additionally, there is no evidence that settlers played an active role in introducing alcohol to the Indians. As a matter of fact, it was commonly believed that booze would make Indians harder to deal with. That was the reasoning behind the Indian Prohibition Act of 1832, which prohibited the sale of alcohol to Indians. The ban was lifted in 1953.

I looked at numerous Native American websites on alcoholism, and all of them pointed to the root causes of alcoholism as occurring within the community. Here is what a woman named Christina wrote in a Facebook discussion entitled, "Is alcoholism white man's fault?":

> I believe that it's the white man who introduced us to alcohol but it's our fault today to continue being alcoholics. Both my parents were alcoholics and drug addicts. I was raised in foster care my whole life and I know that if I get too carried away with partying its way easier for me to become addicted. So it's all a choice, it's not like there's a white man shoving booze down your throat.

The truth is that most Native Americans were initially unaffected by alcohol. They viewed it to be a white man's problem. In fact, this remained true for most tribes up until the 1960s.

I believe the Native Americans' trouble with alcoholism is a direct result of the welfare state. The "Great Society" programs that President Lyndon Johnson introduced have enslaved millions of people to a lifestyle of government dependency. Because welfare eats away at one's self worth, a large number of recipients turn to drugs and alcohol in an effort to forget their problems. Johnson may have meant well, but his "War on Poverty" has been a war on the impoverished.

Native Americans make up about 7 percent of Montana's state

population, but Native American adults receive 40 percent of the state's welfare checks. Most reservations have a wealth of land—yet that land remains largely undeveloped. Even the introduction of gambling has done little to improve the lot of Indians.[64]

I can see why the devil chose to use welfare and alcoholism to enslave Native Americans. According to a report by the North American Mission Board of the Southern Baptist Convention, about 95 percent of the Native American population is unsaved.[65]

Some people have discovered the source of the problem, but their voices aren't loud enough to turn the tide. Herman Whitegrass, a chemical dependency counselor for the Blackfeet tribe in Montana, noted that well-meaning efforts like welfare actually have made things worse. "Some people need the welfare system to get a step up, but other people get stuck in it," Whitegrass said. "I believe the welfare system has disabled us by enabling people to continue their destructive behaviors."[66]

## Black America: Self-Destruction

The welfare system has also had a devastating impact on African Americans. Even though blacks only make up 12 percent of the total population, they comprise 37.2 percent of the people on food stamps.[67]

In the black community, there is a huge problem with crime, drugs, and single parenthood. The murder rate in some cities has exploded in recent years. Young, black males are killing each other at a rate of 36.36 per hundred thousand—nearly seven times the national overall homicide rate of 5.30 per hundred thousand. During one particular weekend, a crime wave swept Chicago, leaving ten dead among fifty-four wounded.[68]

The clearest indication of a demonic plot is the media's cover-up of this issue. It's as if the Ku Klux Klan were to decide it wasn't making any progress and chose to take over the press. Intercity youths are destroying themselves, and the media is almost completely silent about the matter.

A growing mountain of evidence shows that the media is suppressing information about any negative behavior issues in the minority communities. Even in cases of armed robbery, where the race of a suspect is helpful in identifying the perpetrator, the liberal media often withholds this information. (Of course, if the criminal is a white male in his twenties, news organizations seem to have no problem releasing that information.)

In one case, a news station reported that a robbery suspect was a young male who was "either white or Hispanic." Even though the reporter knew the suspect was Hispanic, the story mentioned both races—for no apparent, logical reason.

Just as it is with Native Americans, the politically correct movement has had a genocidal impact on blacks. Before the advent of the "Great Society," blacks had strong family ties. They often lived together in large, extended families. Today, most blacks are raised in single-parent homes. Many have a greater bond with gang members than they do with their own relatives.

Lloyd Marcus, a black leader of the Tea Party movement, gives wonderful insight into the destructive nature of the new racism. He said in a speech that when he was a child, he had been brainwashed into believing that white people were the source of the problem in the black community. But even as a youth, he could see that government dependency was the true source of the problem. He thanked his father for saving his life by moving his family out of the projects, and continued:

Several of my cousins were not as fortunate. They grew up in fatherless homes and [were] on government welfare most of their lives. [The] government provided just enough to keep them dependent. A hand up is a good thing. But, government controlling people via cradle-to-grave dependency is evil. My cousins' lives sucked: drug and alcohol abuse, crime, serial out-of-wedlock births, etc. Many died young.[69]

Black leaders like Jesse Jackson and Al Sharpton have dedicated their lives to defending a system that destroys the people they claim to represent. Sharpton recently called a press conference to condemn an anti-abortion billboard overlooking New York City's Soho district. The sign depicting a young black girl read, "The Most Dangerous Place for an African-American is in the Womb." Sharpton said the message was "classic racial profiling." In one interview, he claimed that taking innocent life in the womb is a civil right.[70]

The reason we have so much racial insanity is that, for the most part, people are afraid to stand for the truth. One of the worst things that could happen to us today would be to be called a "racist." The day is coming when we will be labeled as "racists" for simply claiming to be Christians. If believers could look down the road and see what the devil has planned for us, they would be far more aggressive in fighting for truth.

I truly believe blacks as a whole are more enslaved today than they were before the Civil War. A slave working in a cotton field in the early 1800s may have been in physical bondage. But the fact that he was singing the spiritual lyrics, "swing low, sweet chariot, coming for to carry me home," proved he had found true freedom.

## The Inescapable Debt Trap

The welfare state is very destructive, but limited in scope. A far greater vehicle for economic enslavement is rapidly headed our way. For years, I've read reports from conspiracy theorists who predicted a global cabal was planning on taking over the world by staging a financial crisis. I'm still doubtful that an organized effort is at work, but I do agree that we are headed for a financial crisis.

We have always had concerns about our national debt, but we are now in uncharted territory. The burden has reached a point that it is nearly impossible to manage.

Marc Faber, who publishes the *Gloom, Boom, and Doom Report*, has predicted many of the financial calamities that have occurred in the past few years. He strongly believes we are headed for a debt meltdown:

> I think we are all doomed. I think what will happen is that we are in the midst of a kind of a crack-up boom that is not sustainable, that eventually the economy will deteriorate, that there will be more money-printing, and then you have inflation, and a poor economy, an extreme form of stagflation, and, eventually, in that situation, countries go to war, and, as a whole, derivatives, the market, and everything will collapse, and like a computer when it crashes, you will have to reboot it.[71]

The numbers on our national debt are so huge and are growing so fast that any attempt to cite current figures would quickly date this book. Since we are already past the point of no return in the current monetary system, I think it's more important to focus on what will cause the systemic collapse. Here are five main factors I believe will eventually push us over the edge:

## 1. Running Out of Creditors

In the next decade, the United States Treasury will need to raise at least $10 trillion to cover America's projected fiscal shortfalls. It's a big question whether there will be enough buyers for all this new debt.

China is our largest creditor, and its holdings of U.S. bonds are around $1 trillion. Coming up with ten new Chinas seems like an impossible task. Since our credit-worthiness will only decrease over time, there is just all the less chance of achieving this miracle.

The only alternative for a nation that has run out of creditors is to start loaning money to itself by printing new currency. We are now at that point. The Federal Reserve has managed to prevent a panic by giving the whole process the fancy title of "quantitative easing." However, new verbiage cannot save us from the consequences of what will result: old-fashioned hyperinflation.

## 2. The Debt Load Suppressing Growth

The size of the national debt has become a problem in that it locks up capital that could otherwise be used to grow the economy. And right now, our only option for escaping the debt crisis is to improve the economy. As our nation's gross domestic product (GDP) becomes larger, our ability to service the debt increases. Currently, the debt is growing at 10 percent each year and the

GDP growth rate is at 2.5 percent. This means our projected debt is compounding at a 7.5 percent annual rate.

With trillions of dollars invested in government bonds and Treasury bills, there is little money to invest in the economy. As the debt gets larger, the drain on the economy only becomes stronger. Nominal GDP has only increased at an annual rate of 0.1 percent since 1991. This reality is probably the reason we are having such a slow recovery from the great recession that started in 2008. Eventually, the burden will become so great that the debt will create a hopeless situation by causing the economy to experience negative growth.

## 3. Rising Interest Rates

The Federal Reserve's policy of cheap money has allowed the U.S. to run up huge debt without having high interest payments. The Department of the Treasury has maximized the savings by funding most of our debt with notes that mature in less than five years.

According to the U.S. Treasury's website, the average rate on the debt is around 3.3 percent. Even though our debt has doubled in the last six years, we pay less in interest. We run into a problem if the market drives up the borrowing cost of money. If rates rose to 6 percent, the size of our interest payment would double, resulting in a $2-trillion annual deficit. If rates went to 12 percent, we would have a $3-trillion shortfall.[72]

Several European nations already have been forced into insolvency by spikes in rates. They received bailouts from the International Monetary Fund (IMF) and fellow European Union (EU) members. No nation is large enough to give the U.S. a handout.

## 4. The Loss of Reserve Currency Status

The U.S. dollar has long been the most trusted form of paper currency. After World War II, the Bretton Woods system of monetary management deliberately placed the greenback as the anchor of the global financial system. If a nation wants to buy goods from another nation, it first needs to purchase dollars.[73]

The nonstop process of dollar printing in Washington DC has caused the dollar to slowly lose its appeal as a reserve currency. Central banks don't want their holdings in a currency that can't safeguard value. As the dollar continues to decline in value, it becomes harder for the Treasury to find foreign buyers of our debt.

It would be "game over" for America if the Chinese suddenly declared they were dumping their holdings of U.S. debt. As the financial health of America becomes more questionable, it's going to be difficult to maintain any trust in the dollar.

## 5. Entitlement Programs

It is often said that we need to save our entitlement programs from bankruptcy. What people don't realize is that Social Security and Medicare were insolvent from day one. The money people paid into the system was never saved. The so-called "trust fund" is full of IOUs from Uncle Sam.

Social Security and Medicare are nothing more than giant Ponzi schemes. For several decades, the people drawing from these entitlement programs have been taking more out than they've ever paid in. Several presidents added to the deficit by signing bills that expand coverage.

Now that the baby boom generation is starting to retire, we face a bill that amounts to $100 trillion. We can't fill a hole that is seven times larger than our current GDP. We are at the point that all we can do is buy more time with monetary Band-Aids.

In the coming years, Social Security or Medicare will add hundreds of billions of dollars to the annual deficit. By the year 2030, as few as two people could be paying into the Social Security system for every one person drawing benefits. Since you can't tax 30 percent of someone's income just to pay for retirees, the system is bound to have collapsed before we reach that point.

## Other Key Nations Share the Same Illness

America is not the only nation with a debt problem. Europe and Japan have equally large debt loads. Even oil-rich Arab nations have a problem with runaway deficit spending.

Japan shoulders the biggest public-debt burden among industrialized countries, and because of the size of the Japanese economy, its debt problem needs the most attention.

The size of Japan's debt is a staggering 240 percent of the gross domestic product. To give you a perspective of the size of this financial burden, the U.S. has a national debt that is only at 100 percent of GDP. Japan is able to manage its debt because rates are incredibly low. With a ten-year bond that only pays 1 percent, rates would only have to rise to 2 percent to trigger a Japanese default.

The most likely factor that could trigger a collapse in Japan is its rapidly aging population. With nearly all the debt held by the citizens of that nation, the need to draw upon savings will eventually bankrupt retirement services.

## The Ultimate Economic Enslavement

And he causeth all, both small and great, rich and poor, free and bond, to receive a mark in their right hand, or in their foreheads: And that no man might buy or sell, save he that had the mark, or the name of the beast, or the number of his name. Here is wisdom. Let him that hath understanding count the number of the beast: for it is the number of a man; and his number is Six hundred threescore and six. (Revelation 13:11–18)

Ever since John, the servant of God, wrote the book of Revelation and mentioned the number 666, people have been trying to figure out the meaning of the mark of the Beast. I believe the mark or number of the Beast will be a financial identification system Antichrist will establish during the Tribulation. He will use the mark as a tool for controlling all aspects of society.

Antichrist will make it compulsory for everyone to have a tiny microchip implanted under the skin of the right hand or on the forehead. The microchip will hold data pertaining to each person who receives the implant. Right now, the technology exists to fully implement this system. From here on out, the only likely changes in the technology will involve how much information the microchips will be able to hold.

Everyone who receives the mark will also have to swear allegiance to Antichrist and acknowledge him as the supreme authority. This is why all who take the mark of the Beast will be condemned to hell:

And the third angel followed them, saying with a loud voice, If any man worship the beast and his image, and receive his mark in his forehead, or in his hand, The same shall drink of the wine of the wrath of God, which is poured out without mixture into the cup of his indignation; and he shall be tormented with fire and brimstone in the presence of the holy angels, and in the presence of the Lamb: And the smoke of their torment ascendeth up for ever and ever: and they have no rest day nor night, who worship the beast and his image, and whosoever receiveth the mark of his name. (Revelation 14:9–11)

All who choose not to receive the mark will be unable to buy anything because cash, checks, and credit cards will all be replaced by the Beast system's instant funds. The inability to spend money will require a huge amount of endurance on the part of people who come to faith in Jesus Christ. Someone might have $10 million in the bank, yet be starving to death because he or she refuses to take the mark.

There are some positive ideas for a Tribulation saint to consider. For example, taking the mark of the Beast will result in total enslavement, but the Antichrist's reign will only last for forty-two months. By the end of his rule, little will be left to buy and sell. The Bible says that at the end of the Tribulation, money will become so insignificant that people will cast their silver and gold into the streets.

They shall cast their silver in the streets, and their gold shall be removed: their silver and their gold shall not be able to deliver them in the day of the wrath of the LORD: they shall not satisfy their souls, neither fill their bowels: because it is the stumbling block of their iniquity. (Ezekiel 7:19)

Money cannot save a slave or a master from God's judgment. If someone is to be eternally free, he or she needs to trust in Jesus Christ. He paid the price of liberty to free us from the bondage of sin:

**Acts 4:12:** And there is salvation in no one else; for there is no other name under heaven that has been given among men by which we must be saved.

**Matthew 10:22:** And ye shall be hated of all [men] for my name's sake: but he that endureth to the end shall be saved.

chapter seven

# ECONOMIC COLLAPSE

*What a Difference a Day Makes*

*By Tony Burtovoy II*

I N THIS CHAPTER, we'll discuss some of the dynamics of a few real-life economies in recent times that have collapsed under fiat money systems. We'll observe how and why they collapsed, the speed of collapse, and how greed, corruption, and sin in political leadership always eventually result in disaster—often with surprising suddenness. Throughout this chapter, it will become apparent that corruption and sin in the halls of economic authority is dangerous, at least…but perhaps even inspired by ungodly influences. Before we get into some specific examples, let us build up to that point by examining a few historical moments from a biblical perspective.

From Luke chapter 4:

> And the devil, taking him up into an high mountain,
> shewed unto him all the kingdoms of the world in a

moment of time. And the devil said unto him, All this power will I give thee, and the glory of them: for that is delivered unto me; and to whomsoever I will, I give it. If thou therefore wilt worship me, all shall be thine.

And Jesus answered and said unto him, Get thee behind me, Satan: for it is written, Thou shalt worship the Lord thy God, and him only shalt thou serve…. And when the devil had ended all the temptation, he departed from him for a season. (Luke 4:5–8, 13)

About the words, "for that is delivered unto me; and to whomsoever I will, I give it," what a proclamation! It's a statement full of secondary meaning. Satan seems to be saying that at some point before AD 27–30 (the commonly held window for the most probable beginning of Jesus' ministry on earth), he was awarded authority over all earthly kingdoms. This is easy enough to believe, considering the violent and sinful nature of ancient kingdoms. However, Satan is not keeping this authority to himself; he seems to be actively seeking someone on earth to whom to give his power and authority. Why? Perhaps he is not currently allowed to act physically in the earthly realm until the time when God allows him to do so. Whatever the case, we'll not dwell on that right now. For now, it will be interesting enough to focus on Satan's authority over the kingdoms of the earth throughout the centuries.

If we assume that Satan occasionally—or even frequently— seeks to give his authority to mortals, we can reasonably guess his motive: "control." Certainly, Satan bestows authority only in exchange for promises of worship—and by extension, influence and control in the resulting human society. This is precisely what he offered Christ during the temptation in the wilderness.

Satan wants to control the affairs of mankind. He wants to be the recipient of the worship only due to God, and he wants to replace God. We know from the words in Luke that Christ denied Satan's offer. Accordingly, we should probably assume that sometime after departing from Jesus, Satan probably found someone else to whom to give his authority. Whether days or decades later, that person or group probably assumed some level of power and either continued to hold that power across long stretches of time or fell and lost that power. Although this is speculation based on logic, there have been haunting clues over the last two thousand years about secret societies and secretive groups with vast wealth and international influence, as well as about very powerful people who seem to be outside of national consideration, structure, and law. For the purposes of this work, let us not focus on whether such people really exist or who they might be. Instead, we will zero in on a few of the economic tactics often implemented in earthly kingdoms—tactics that may very well be satanically inspired.

## Money

While it doesn't likely need much further definition at this point, remember that money, in basic terms, is simply a standardized means of payment for goods and services. Historically, money has been implemented using valuable commodities like gold and silver. Over time, governments have moved largely to the use of fiat money instead of valuable or rare materials. *It is important to realize that every fiat money system ever implemented in the history of the world has collapsed in disaster.* Surprising? Are there any particular reasons fiat money systems are prone to abuse and collapse?

## Fiat Money

"Fiat" is a term derived from a Latin word meaning "let it be done" and describes economic systems in which money is given value by law or decree. It is a substitute of something with little or no value for something of actual value. In modern times in the United States, the dollar is the "fiat" currency. Fiat money like the dollar has no real value except for that which the local government says it has. It's little more than pressed cotton, ink, strands of fibers, security stripes, protective glazes, and other chemicals. According to the Bretton Woods system of international monetary exchange, shortly after World War II, the dollar was valued—by decree—at one thirty-fifth of an ounce of pure gold. This was a sneaky way of proclaiming that gold was to immediately change value to thirty-five dollars an ounce overnight.

Many kingdoms of ages past have also proclaimed decrees like this and have implemented and abused fiat currencies. Remember, every fiat currency system in the history of the world has collapsed in disaster. It's plausible, then, to speculate that no human government has ever been able to resist the temptation to create wealth by abusing fiat money. Hearken back to Luke chapter 4: Jesus didn't hesitate to deny Satan's offer. However, it's apparent that mortal men cannot resist such temptations.

So, just how is wealth created and abused in a fiat money system? For better or worse, it's created by devaluing the fiat. In a paper-note fiat system, it's accomplished basically by printing more dollars. Overprinting or excessive debasement can be considered as abuse because for every dollar printed, each one still in circulation becomes worth slightly less. This is not apparent on the surface, because a dollar is always worth one hundred pennies. However, this is easily seen when the prices of goods and services begin to rise because of the abuse. This always occurs during periods of fiat debasement, and the road to collapse becomes only a matter of mathematics and time once the debasement begins.

## Fractional-Reserve Banking

Many kingdoms of ages past have also used systems like the modern *fractional-reserve* banking system. Under this concept, a bank only needs to keep enough cash on hand to meet a percentage requirement set by the governing authority. The bank, in essence, is allowed to use money, loan it out, and get interest payments in return without any investment (or risk) of their own resources. As long as all the owners of the money don't withdraw from their accounts at the same time, there is no problem. This is a clear example of greedy, corrupt people who've given themselves over to sin, greedy lust, and evil economic practices. They are unable to resist the temptation to grab at the illusion of wealth and power—unlike Christ in the wilderness. This seems completely normal to men of such wicked caliber: "Woe unto them that call evil good, and good evil; that put darkness for light, and light for darkness; that put bitter for sweet, and sweet for bitter!" (Isaiah 5:20).

The fractional-reserve system is not just a modern concept. Here's an example that occurred well before recent times:

The Florentine banking houses had begun to lend out money held in demand deposits in the late thirteenth and early fourteenth centur[ies], which created a sizable economic boom. When early in the fourteenth century,

Neapolitan princes began to withdraw funds and England was found incapable of repaying loans it had received from these banks, the artificial boom could no longer be sustained. In addition, the public debt of Florence had been financed by speculative bank loans, and the value of these government bonds also began to decline dramatically.

The entire Florentine banking industry went under between 1341 and 1346, with depositors getting back only between one-fifth to one-half of their deposited funds, after a long waiting period. Moreover, a credit shortage developed, which in turn led to the failure of many other businesses as well. The inflationary boom had turned to bust.

A similar fate awaited the famous Medici Bank in the late fifteenth century. Initially, the bank was not a deposit bank, but only accepted money on loan.

However, it then began to accept demand deposits as well, and soon **yielded to the temptation** of lending them out. Its reserve ratio had fallen to 50 percent of its deposit liabilities when the artificial inflationary boom began to falter, and during the inevitable recession, this ratio fell to as low as 10 percent. The bank, and most of its competitors at the time, naturally failed.[74]

It's interesting that the author of this article uses the same phrase, "yielded to temptation," that we've been focusing on thus far. No one except Christ alone is moral enough or powerful enough to resist this temptation. The creation of artificial wealth through sinful means is explicitly denounced in the Bible: "If thou lend money to any of my people that is poor by thee, thou shalt not be to him as an usurer, neither shalt thou lay upon him usury" (Exodus 22:25).

Usury, or interest, is not only burdensome for the borrower, but can drag the lender down with temptation and corruption:

> And if thy brother be waxen poor, and fallen in decay with thee; then thou shalt relieve him: yea, though he be a stranger, or a sojourner; that he may live with thee. Take thou no usury of him, or increase: but fear thy God; that thy brother may live with thee. Thou shalt not give him thy money upon usury, nor lend him thy victuals for increase. (Leviticus 25:35–37)

> He that putteth not out his money to usury, nor taketh reward against the innocent. He that doeth these things shall never be moved. (Psalm 15:5)

Now that we've discovered some interesting viewpoints on a few historical biblical moments and have quickly reviewed some peculiar, if not wicked, economic habits of the kingdoms of men, let us examine closely five recent collapses of fiat money systems to try to learn a little bit more.

## Fiat Collapses in Modern Times

### Wiemar Republic, Germany 1919–1923

The Weimar Republic is the name given to the parliamentary system of government in Germany from 1919–1923. It's quite famous as perhaps the most vivid example in modern times of a fiat money system collapsing catastrophically. We'll quote from a simple external source for some specifics and comment along the way.

> In order to pay the large costs of World War I, Germany suspended the convertibility of its currency into gold when that war broke out....
>
> The Treaty of Versailles, however, accelerated the decline in the value of the mark, so that by the end of 1919 more than forty-seven paper marks were required to buy one U.S. dollar....
>
> The result was that the exchange rate of the mark against the U.S. dollar fell steadily throughout the war.... The German currency was relatively stable at about sixty marks per U.S. dollar during the first half of 1921....
>
> The first payment [of war reparations] was paid when due in June 1921. That was the beginning of an increasingly rapid devaluation of the mark, which fell to less than one-third of a cent by November 1921 (approx. 330 marks per U.S. dollar). The total reparations demanded was...(132 billion) goldmarks....
>
> It is sometimes argued that Germany had to **inflate** [the code word for "print more paper notes and use them to pay debt"] its currency to pay the war reparations required under the Treaty of Versailles, but this is misleading, because the Reparations Commission required payment to be in gold marks or in foreign currency, not in the rapidly depreciating paper mark.[75]

This article describes the irresistible temptation to falsely create wealth or to create false wealth. No government in history has resisted the temptation to create false wealth in this manner—whether under outside pressure, as in Weimar, or otherwise.

> During the first half of 1922, the mark stabilized at about 320 marks per dollar accompanied by international reparations conferences, including one in June 1922 organized by U.S. investment banker J. P. Morgan Jr. When these meetings produced no workable solution, the inflation changed to hyperinflation and the mark fell to eight thousand marks per dollar by December 1922. The cost-of-living index was 41 in June 1922 and 685 in December, an increase of more than sixteen times.[76]

This would be equivalent—in terms of the modern U.S. dollar—to all goods and services required for daily living increasing, on average, sixteen times in just six months. That's about a 1.4 percent DAILY cost increase of every single thing you buy every single day for six months. How would you be feeling thirty days into that? Sixty days in? One hundred days? Longer? Think of that $3-a-gallon gasoline purchased in the summer steadily increasing to $48 per gallon right around Christmas! Bread that cost about $2 would increase to $32, a $4.50 package of cheese would spike to $72, and a $3 jug of milk would climb to $48. If you were a typical family that spent about $120 each week on groceries, would you be able to afford an increase of $1,920 per week just to eat?

Living under this kind of economic crisis is impossible. People formerly blind to such economic blunders that lead to these kinds of busts are catapulted into action against further degradation. The common result is monetary resetting or outright replacement of currencies. All of this causes large portions (if not all) of the false wealth to be erased from history. People once thought of as wealthy soon realize that much of what they thought they had was actually just an illusion. Not often realized is the speed at which this can occur. Collapses can seem to go slowly for some time, but at those moments of critical mass, they can become catastrophic on a monthly, weekly, or even daily basis. All this is the direct result of abusing the fiat money-printing system. In the short term, it appears to increase wealth—but only in the size of the numbers! Once the slide in value begins, it is VERY difficult to turn around. The devaluation at some point causes the value of the fiat notes to plummet, in turn prompting the prices of commodities to rise sharply in the reverse direction. This creates panic in economic markets and among the citizenry, which only makes things worse as people rush to get rid of their paper notes. Panic can lead to all sorts of disastrous consequences. In fact, as stated in chapter two, "hyperinflation is widely believed to have contributed to the Nazi takeover of Germany and Adolf Hitler's rise to power."[77]

## Analysis of the Wiemar Republic Example

The German fiat money system during the years of Weimar was unstable at best. Losing the war and being hit with reparations certainly made matters worse. Germany was not required to pay reparations with paper money, but did yield to temptation to do so via a scheme to buy foreign exchanges with fiat paper, backed by treasuries and commercial debt. This backfired and sped the decline. During the last half of 1923, the speed of the collapse was so fast that the cost-of-living index increased sixteen times within six months. German leadership during this era made ill-advised economic decisions on a foundation of a dangerous fiat money system that was already in trouble. This resulted in the destruction of the money system, the liquidation of the wealth of millions of people, and great suffering and hardship of millions of citizens. It possibly even laid the groundwork for a second great war within a decade. The danger of fiat money, false-wealth creation, and control mechanisms go far beyond one or two levels. Mankind's inability to resist the temptations of satanic-like wealth and power is a recipe for continuation of the boom/bust cycle, as well as the sin and suffering associated with each.

$$\$\,\$\,\$$

Apart from Weimar, the classic example on this topic, let us look very briefly at four other modern fiat money systems that collapsed speedily in modern times. Since much analysis has already been completed by now via the Weimar example, we'll spend less time on these next examples and avoid stating too many similar points. Keep in mind, however, how "basis in fiat" and the inability to resist temptation to create false wealth are always in play. When a crisis comes along, the fiat money system and the hidden economic sins attached to it very often boil to the surface rapidly and cause the system to expose its sinful nature, collapse suddenly, and cause great suffering to those living under its implied mechanism of *economic control.*

## Bosnia, 1993

The breakup of the Soviet Union in 1989 yielded a new nation in the area of former Yugoslavia.

Bosnia and Herzegovina went through its worst inflation in 1993. In 1992, the highest denomination was one thousand dinara. By 1993, the highest denomination was one hundred million dinara. In the Republika Srpska, the highest denomination was ten thousand dinara in 1992 and ten billion dinara in 1993. Fifty billion dinara notes were also printed in 1993 but never issued.[78]

The period of Bosnian hyperinflation during 1993–1994 has been referred to as the worst episode of hyperinflation in history. After breaking away from the Soviet Union, the Communist Party in Bosnia became more and more irrational in its economic policy. In simplest terms, it **yielded to the temptation** of printing money rather than soundly growing the nation via economics and production. After a short while, it also added more and more restrictions on citizens' access to their own savings, allowing the government to loot the nation's wealth. From late 1993 to early 1995, prices in this nation grew by 5 quadrillion percent. The following snippets from an insightful article describe this scene perfectly:

> The government operated a network of stores at which goods were supposed to be available at artificially low prices. In practice these stores seldom had anything to sell....
>
> All of the government gasoline stations eventually were closed and gasoline was available only from roadside dealers whose operation consisted of a car parked with a plastic can of gasoline sitting on the hood....
>
> Most car owners gave up driving and relied upon

public transportation. But the Belgrade transit authority…did not have the funds necessary for keeping its fleet
of twelve hundred buses operating.…

Despite the government's desperate printing of
money, it still did not have the funds to keep the infra-
structure in operation.[79]

The government became desperate in its attempts to print
money. Again, it **yielded to the temptation** to create false wealth
in order to delay the inevitable a little bit longer. It had obviously
been abusing the fiat system before this time—and once the problems gained momentum, the government was trapped. It could
let the fiat system collapse immediately and have its money-printing crimes exposed, or it could print even more money and delay
the collapse. The second choice let the government "live outside
of prison" for a little while longer but increased the suffering of
the nation later when the collapse finally came, when hyperinflation was so much worse.

Potholes developed in the streets, elevators stopped func-
tioning, and construction projects were closed down. The
unemployment rate exceeded 30 percent.…

The government tried to counter the inflation by
imposing price controls. But when inflation continued,
the government price controls made the price producers
were getting so ridiculously low that they simply stopped
producing. In October of 1993, the bakers stopped making bread.…

In October of 1993 [the government] created a new
currency unit. One new dinar was worth one million of

the "old" dinars. In effect, the government simply removed six zeroes from the paper money. This, of course, did not stop the inflation.[80]

## Analysis of the Bosnia Example

The chain of events here is amazing! A fiat paper system, shaky by nature, was troubled by the political trauma of the Soviet breakup in 1989 and shocked into crisis by war. This is similar to Weimar and most other fiat collapses. The economic authority becomes reckless with a system that's already shaky and **yields to the temptation** to create false wealth in hopes that the flawed fiat money system in place will be able to withstand the crime for just a little while longer. Interesting in this example is the human element. People simply stopped producing rather than making mandated business transactions. The speed of collapse in Bosnia also attests to the premise about how fast these events can occur. When critical mass is reached, the inflationary pressures become exponential. Even the unwillingness of the citizenry to participate in the slide can make it go faster.

## Russia, 1998

The buildup to the August 17, 1998, Russian financial collapse is not very different than other fiat money system implosions of modern times. The Russian ruble had been on shaky ground since the breakup of the Soviet Union in 1989. Poor productivity of industrial sectors adjusting to a post-Soviet world and frequent political turmoil set the stage for the shock that was soon to come. As with other modern fiats, when they are abused and weak, a shock to the system often sends them reeling. In this case, the Asian financial crisis of 1997 did the trick. During the course of events:

> Political crisis came to a head in March when Russian president Boris Yeltsin suddenly dismissed Prime Minister Viktor Chernomyrdin and his entire cabinet on March 23....
>
> The growth of internal loans could only be provided at the expense of the inflow of foreign speculative capital, which was attracted by very high interest rates: In an effort to prop up the currency and stem the flight of capital, in June Kiriyenko hiked GKO [an abbreviation for government bonds issued by the state of Russia] interest rates to 150 percent. The situation was worsened by irregular internal debt payments. Despite government efforts, the debts on wages continued to grow, especially in the remote regions. By the end of 1997, the situation with the tax receipts was very tense, and it had a negative effect on the financing of the major budget items (pensions, communal utilities, transportation, etc.)....
>
> The inability of the Russian government to implement a coherent set of economic reforms led to a severe erosion in investor confidence and a chain reaction that can be likened to a run on the Central Bank.[81]

We know exactly why "runs" on a bank are bad in a fiat or reserve money system: The majority of money thought to be on deposit is not really there!

On August 13, 1998, the Russian stock, bond, and currency markets collapsed as a result of investor fears that the government would devalue the ruble, default on domestic debt, or both. Annual yields on ruble-denominated bonds were more than 200 percent. The stock market had to be closed for thirty-five minutes as prices plummeted. When the market closed, it was down 65 percent with a small number of shares actually traded. From January to August, the stock market had lost more than 75 percent of its value, 39 percent in the month of May alone....

On August 17, 1998, the Russian government devalue[d] the ruble, default[ed] on domestic debt, and declare[d] a moratorium on payment to foreign creditors.[82]

This speaks to our premise of speedy collapse. In a single moment, after the government is trapped into doing so after years of temptation to print excessive paper notes and corrosive abuse of reserve banking, the paper system is devalued, which wipes out much of the falsely created money.

Russian inflation in 1998 reached 84 percent and welfare costs grew considerably. Many banks were closed down as a result of the crisis....

Prices for almost all Russian food items had gone up by almost 100 percent, while imports had quadrupled in price. Many citizens were stocking up for bad times and throughout the country, shop shelves were being emptied, leaving a shortage of even the most basic items.... The crisis also increased social tension…millions of people lost their life savings from the bank closures.[83]

## Analysis of the Russian Example

Here we have yet again hyperinflated prices and loss of the wealth of the people in order to wash out the crimes of the abusive and wicked people who fiddle with economic controls for their own pleasures and agendas. The Russian collapse is interesting, however, because of the nation's former superpower status. Russia was also heavily tied into commodities like oil, natural gas, metal, and timber. The shock of the Asian financial crisis and commodity declines hit hard at the outset and was enough to alarm their system to its core. However, with its vast land area and natural resources, recovery occurred relatively quickly when commodity prices rebounded. As well, Russia's powerful status on the world scene encouraged capital infusions after some time. Even with the quick recovery, millions of people lost their life savings during the collapse, and suffering was great. Those mortals at the economic helm, like their modern counterparts elsewhere in this study, were incapable of resisting the unabashed theft of wealth in this way and were unable to stand firm against the temptation for gain of such power and riches. Will it happen again in Russia? Since no fiat money system in the history of the world has survived without disastrous collapse, the answer to that question is most certainly "Yes!"

## Zimbabwe, 2000–present

Zimbabwe's hyperinflation began in the early 2000s after political instability, controversial confiscation of white-owned farmland by the government, and difficulties with debts to the International Monetary Fund (IMF). At present, that nation's hyperinflation rates are astounding. In late 2008, it was estimated at 89.7 sextillion percent (that is 89.7 times ten—with twenty-one zeroes). At the end of 2008, it was 6.5 quindecillion percent (that is 6.5 times ten—with 108 zeroes). This is far beyond what the human mind can imagine. At present, Zimbabwean currency is no longer even printed!

> Early in the twenty-first century, Zimbabwe started to experience hyperinflation. Inflation reached 624 percent in early 2004, then fell back to low triple digits….
>
> On 16 February 2006…the government had printed ZWD [the currency abbreviation for the Zimbabwe dollar] 21trillion in order to buy foreign currency to pay off IMF arrears….
>
> In early May 2006, Zimbabwe's government began printing money again to produce about 60 trillion Zimbabwean dollars.[84]

The progression of collapse here is very fast and fits well with our assertion that these things can get out of control very quickly. The economic authority in Zimbabwe **yielded to temptation** to abuse its fiat money system to its fullest and most horrific extreme right from the outset. This looting of the nation's wealth was complete and undeniable from a very early stage.

> In August 2006, the Zimbabwean government issued new currency and asked citizens to turn in old notes; the new currency…had three zeroes slashed from it…. In

February 2007, the central bank of Zimbabwe declared inflation "illegal," outlawing any raise in prices on certain commodities between March 1 and June 30, 2007.[85]

Here we see price controls instituted by a government doing too little too late, just as in other fiat collapses. Price controls don't work because the citizenry either disobeys them, operates in black markets, or simply stops producing goods. The misery caused by this was certainly horrific.

The Reserve Bank of Zimbabwe issued a ZWD 10-million note in January 2008, roughly equivalent of four U.S. dollars. Zimbabwe's inflation soared to a record high of 26,470.8 percent.[86]

At this point, the progression of collapse is becoming almost too much to comprehend. Zimbabwe was not a rich nation by any means before this event, and this situation very quickly turned into a misery fest for the record books.

By the beginning of July 2008, official figures put the inflation rate at 355,000 percent...with some independent estimates as high as 8.5 million percent.... On July 16, the official inflation rate was...2.2 million percent....
On 19 July 2008, the Reserve Bank of Zimbabwe announced plans to introduce a one-hundred-billion bank note....
On July 30, 2008, the governor of the RBZ [Reserve Bank of Zimbabwe]...announced that the Zimbabwe dollar would be redenominated by removing ten zeroes....

ZWD ten billion [would] become one dollar after the redenomination.[87]

Just as in other modern fiat catastrophes, the economic authority being trapped with no tools left to squeeze any more juice out of the imploded fiat system executes a monetary reset. This essentially crosses out some zeros on the paper notes. What it does in reality is wipe out some of the falsely created wealth in those notes so that the resulting ratios are closer to the truth of how much value is really in the system. This is little more than covering up the crime of overprinting the fiat currency in the first place.

On 17 November 2008, Johns Hopkins University Professor Steve H. Hanke released a document estimating Zimbabwe's annualized and monthly inflation rates were 89.7 sextillion percent and 79.6 billion percent, respectively, as of 14 November 2008…. According to Prof. Hanke's calculations, prices in Zimbabwe increased roughly sixty-four times between 7 November and 14 November….

On December 6, 2008, the Reserve Bank of Zimbabwe announced plans to circulate the ZWD two-hundred-million note, just days after introducing the ZWD one-hundred-million note. Even with the circulation of both notes amid the entrenched hyperinflation, the Reserve Bank of Zimbabwe left in place caps on daily cash withdrawals at five hundred thousand Zimbabwe dollars, which is the equivalent of about twenty-five U.S. cents….

On 12 January 2009, Zimbabwe introduced the fifty-billion note….

On January 16, 2009, Zimbabwe announced plans for imminent issue of banknotes of $10 trillion, $20 trillion, $50 trillion, and $100 trillion. At the time of the announcement, the last was valued at around thirty U.S. dollars, but that value was expected to evaporate swiftly....

In February, the government of Zimbabwe revalued its currency. One of these new Zimbabwean dollars is worth one trillion of the previous. This move took the number of decimal places removed during the period of hyperinflation to twenty-five.[88]

## Analysis of the Zimbabwe Example

Well, if you stuck with the story of Zimbabwe through all that and you understand even just a little bit about math, then you're probably picking your jaw up off the floor right about now. The fiat system in Zimbabwe collapsed catastrophically—of that there is no doubt. The government during this period refused to resist the temptation to print money to such a degree that it ensured that the economy as it was will NEVER recover from that kind of debt and will keep its people in misery for years. The speed of the decline was astounding at times. At one point, in just ONE HOUR, a single bottle of beer increased in price by fifty billion Zimbabwean dollars!

## Argentina, 1980s–present

Here's a sobering fact: Argentina has been bailed out in one way or another nine times since 1983. Here's another: The 1992 peso equals one hundred billion pre-1983 pesos. That's classic hyper-inflation brought on by the printing of excess paper money in a fiat money system.

> Argentina's shaky economy is rooted in its dependent role in a world economy dominated by the imperialist countries. Although it is the third-biggest economy in Latin America and trade is only 10 percent of its economic output, Argentina isn't immune from the perpetual current account shortfalls in its external balance of payments....
>
> Like many of its third-world counterparts, Argentina plugged these shortfalls by external borrowing, most of it in U.S. dollars. The interest payments became crushing when the U.S. raised its interest rates...in the late 1970s, [precipitating] massive defaults on external debt by dozens of third-world countries in the early 1980s.... Banks, corporations, and governments that were holding most of these debts were not going to let these countries not "honor" the debt....
>
> The creditors...coerce[d] poor countries into "restructuring" the debts, often on the condition that they implement extensive privatization ("market opening")....
>
> The drying up of foreign investment after 1982, and the Argentine government's recourse to printing more money to meet its spending needs, laid the foundation for Argentina's hyperinflation—up to 5,000 percent in the late 1980s.[89]

There it is! The government's "recourse to printing more money" becomes reality as the only way out of a desperate situation. In this last example, we find yet again that nugget of temptation and man's inability to escape its clutches. Granted, this was essentially an emergency situation and the government was pressured into taking this route, but in this and every case throughout history, it only occurred after previous abuse and fiat money printing, which caused the systems to be overloaded with falsely created currency units. When a crisis eventually came, in each case, the government had no choice but to destroy each financial system by overprinting money. The inability of men to resist the temptation to create false wealth certainly occurs before the "recourse to print more money" comes about. All historical kingdoms, as well as Argentina, were living beyond their means on money that did not exist.

> In the fifteen years since 1975...inflation averaged 300 percent.... Argentina's economy contracted by more than 10 percent in the 1980s, amid serious capital flight and a sharp deterioration in its terms of trade. Rampant speculation by imperialist banks and fund managers, often targeting Third-World currencies, greatly magnified Argentina's balance-of-payment problem.[90]

Outside pressure from foreign financial speculators certainly contributed to the lead-up to that point of critical mass, when the collapse transitioned from gradual to speedy. Additional outside pressures came in the form of the strengthening dollar and economic turmoil in nearby economies with similar currencies. All of these pressures supported the Argentinean collapse, as outside pressures usually do with unstable fiat systems.

The pegging of the peso to the dollar in 1991 provided a superficial anchor. It would have worked if Argentina's economy moved at much the same tempo as [that of the U.S.]. But it did not (and cannot), so when the dollar strengthened (from the mid-1990s), Argentina was hit hard, and its ability to service its foreign debt was undermined further. The Mexican crisis of 1994–95 and Brazil's devaluation in 1999 made things worse.[91]

## Analysis of the Argentina Example

Argentina experienced many of the same problems as other kingdoms in recent times that have gone through collapse of their fiat money systems. They all typically had questionable leadership for long periods of time. These leaders took grave advantage of the nature of fiat money and reserve banking in order to enrich themselves and control and loot the people of their respective nations. It's likely that some of the governments were cornered into printing excessive money through external pressure (while some were not), but it's certainly true that the abuse of unstable economic models over periods of time caused such a state of weakness that the nations cannot withstand a large shock when it comes. If and when a sufficient shock comes, the whole economic illusion comes crashing down, and everyone under the umbrella of that system suffers great misery, poverty, and sometimes even death. Argentina seems to be in perpetual crisis and, as mentioned earlier, has been bailed out many times in only a short window of recent history. Continued abuse of fiat money ensures that more collapses will come; unless people of character can step forward, learn the example of Christ, take strength through Christ in faith, and resist Satan's temptations to chase after the monetary illusions of this world

# Closing

As Christians, we believe in the validity of the Bible. We accept its words—even if we don't always understand them. We trust that God will reveal meanings as we require and as we persist seeking to know and understand Him. By accepting the words in Scripture, we accept that Christ defeated Satan and death, and that the events of the Gospels are true. Satan proclaimed in Luke chapter 4 that all authority was given to him, and that he could give it to whomever he chose. If Satan is actively influencing human civilization by awarding power and privilege to those who knowingly or unknowingly serve him, then we should consider the possibility that at times throughout human history, evil men may occasionally make their way into positions of power in various kingdoms. We should also consider the possibility that these evil men may knowingly be influenced by Satan somehow, and may cooperate with otherworldly agendas as a return for the gift of power—perhaps even implementing money systems and other systems of control for some macro-generational purpose. This leads to the conclusion that satanic principles for control of large populations within ordered and centralized structures may have been part of human kingdoms for a very long time—two thousand years at least, and maybe longer. We can only speculate about the purpose of this, but the book of Revelation certainly alludes to some possibilities.

If satanic principles are in play in modern society in order to control large populations and ultimately steer them into sin, disaster, and collapse, then we as Christians need to be ever vigilant as to how we conduct our affairs, economic and otherwise. We should exercise godly principles at all times concerning material wealth, debt, and frivolous living. Interpretation of the Word as to how this applies to each Christian is for every individual to discover and apply. We have godly laws for our lives, of course, but these are not meant to enslave us to regulation; they are meant to lead us to Christ and free us from sin!

> And it came to pass, that he went through the corn fields on the sabbath day; and his disciples began, as they went, to pluck the ears of corn. And the Pharisees said unto him, Behold, why do they on the sabbath day that which is not lawful?… And he said unto them, The sabbath was made for man, and not man for the sabbath: Therefore the Son of man is Lord also of the sabbath. (Mark 2:23–24, 27)

The user manual for earthly life has been written! Pray for understanding, then read and apply what the Holy Spirit teaches. God is as much a rewarder of persistence and faith as He is a deliverer of justice to those who reject the free gift of salvation through Christ. Seek Him first and He will never fail you.

## chapter eight

# THE STOCK MARKET

## A Casino without Comps

*By C. H. Gruyère*

IT HAS BEEN 220 years since the enterprising men of the New World started trading ownership interest in companies under the buttonwood tree in lower Manhattan on the corner of Wall and Broad streets. What started as an efficient means of raising capital for all ventures public and private has morphed into a place of mischief, misdeeds, treachery, intrigue, lawlessness, and manipulation. A crime scene. What was once the productive means of allocating capital has become the preferred means of looting the public in ever more creative and confusing ways. The players remain the same, and their motives remain the same. Only now, they even own the cops who are supposed to police them and protect the investing public from their misdeeds. Wall Street companies are the largest contributors to financial campaigns. Wall Street bankers permeate the highest levels of government and currently occupy more high-ranking positions than during any other time in history. Indeed, the current U.S. president has appointed more multimillionaire bankers than one can easily keep track of. Their influence is obvious to anyone who cares to spend even a few moments researching their filthy trail of activity. Their aim is not to uphold the U.S. Constitution or protect the common man of Main Street; it is to carry out a conquest of the people, the nation, and, ultimately, the world. They will get their reward, and they will not like it.

## Proverbs 11:1

"A false balance is abomination to the Lord:
but a just weight is his delight."

One cannot discuss the equity and debt markets (stocks and bonds) without first understanding the nefarious intentions of the extremely unconstitutional Federal Reserve and the dishonest, debt-based money system it has been allowed to run in this country. That topic has been covered skillfully in another chapter of this book. Note well that in ninety-seven years of the Fed's existence, our dollar has lost 97 percent of its original value. Perhaps the goal is to destroy 100 percent of the value by the time it celebrates its one-hundredth anniversary?

The Federal Reserve, which is neither "federal" nor a "reserve," exists to manage booms and busts in the markets so its members can take advantage of citizens and governments. It does this through managing the amount of money that is in circulation. When more money is in motion during boom times, many borrowers expand their businesses, real estate holdings, and investment portfolios. When less money is in circulation and loans get called in, portfolios shrink, local banks go bust, and the "too-big-to-jail" banks who are members of the Fed just happen to be there to "help" by confiscating the smaller banks, larger businesses, and any real estate that suits their fancy. Dollar-denominated currency only has value by decree (fiat). It is created at the push of a button—whether it is the button on a printing press or on a computer. It is issued and destroyed at the whim of the Federal Reserve (cartel). Fiat represents no real labor, no rarity, and no intrinsic value. It only has value because of the confidence placed in it. Furthermore, it is loaned into existence by the cartel, with interest! Yes, the U.S. Constitution clearly gave control of the money system to Congress, to the people. However, unknowing and even unscrupulous politicians abdicated that responsibility to the private banking cartel known as the Federal Reserve. It is no coincidence that there was never an income tax until the year this cartel was founded.

## The Best Slave to Have Is One Who Thinks He Is Free

U.S. citizens give this cartel the raw materials to fabricate currency at will. Then the cartel lends it back to the U.S. citizens with interest. Income taxes pay for that interest and make the cartel wealthy beyond human comprehension. Forget the fact that the Sixteenth Amendment was never legally ratified, and therefore the income tax is not a legally binding obligation. Why are citizens borrowing something that is already theirs? Furthermore, why are the largest institutions and wealthiest businessmen and bankers largely exempt from this cartel's tax? What about the hidden tax of the inflation of the money supply? Do many citizens understand that the value of the dollars in their pockets trends downward year after year? The public has been trained to think in terms of constant dollars. The markets are quoted in fiat currency without regard to the indexed value of that currency. The dollar index is a measure of the U.S. dollar against a basket of six other currencies. In the last ten years, that index has dropped 40 percent.

Now, think about the value of the Dow Jones Industrial Average (DJIA) and what its chart would look like if the 40 percent drop in the value of the dollar were reflected. Putting a number to it, the DJIA would need to be at 36,000 to equal its peak value back in the year 2000. At this writing, it is one-third of that. Now, price the DJIA in something that was regarded as real currency until a few short decades ago, something that has had intrinsic value for thousands of years: gold. If you price the DJIA in gold, you will see that eleven years after its peak in March of 2000, it has lost 82 percent of its value! Now how rich do you feel? The cartel can't have its subjects knowing about this secret tax; they are happy to have the debt slaves distracted with anger about government spending, income taxes, financial markets, and the sham of a political system they find themselves in. "Please don't let them understand how the world really works, don't let them know about the man behind the curtain at the end of the yellow brick road, the Wizard of Ounces!"

The wicked in his pride doth persecute the poor: let them be taken in the devices that they have imagined. For the wicked boasteth of his heart's desire, and blesseth the covetous, whom the LORD abhorreth. The wicked, through the pride of his countenance, will not seek after God: God is not in all his thoughts. His ways are always grievous; thy judgments are far above out of his sight: as for all his enemies, he puffeth at them. He hath said in his heart, I shall not be moved: for I shall never be in adversity. His mouth is full of cursing and deceit and fraud: under his tongue is mischief and vanity. He sitteth in the lurking places of the villages: in the secret places doth he murder the innocent: his eyes are privily set against the poor. He lieth in wait secretly as a lion in his den: he lieth in wait to catch the poor: he doth catch the poor, when he draweth him into his net. He croucheth, and humbleth himself, that the poor may fall by his strong ones. He hath said in his heart, God hath forgotten: he hideth his face; he will never see it. (Psalm 10:2–11)

## Where Are the Adults?

The Glass-Steagall Act (GSA) of 1933 was enacted in the wake of the 1929 stock market crash to prevent banks from using deposits to support a failed underwriting. Banks had taken too much risk in the stock market with depositors' money. They would make a risky loan to a fledgling company, buy shares in that company, then encourage depositors to do the same. The share price would rise due to the artificially created demand, and the bank could sell its shares to depositors for a tidy profit. Oh, don't forget: Back then it was OK for the bank to "park" customer deposits in those very same shares. Now, banks use free money from the cartel to pump up share prices, let the insiders off at the top floor—while the average investor pumps more money into the market by way of 401(k)s, etc.—and if it doesn't work out in their favor, they take depositor money *after* the fact anyway. The moral hazard is that the viability of particular institutions is protected. No free-market capitalism occurs. Rather, greater risk-taking is encouraged as the "too-big-to-fail" institution knows it gets to keep its profits (usually minus a small toll, aka a fine), but large losses will be nationalized (taxpayer bailouts). Compensation arrangements for these companies and the mutual-fund and hedge-fund managers who trade them are heavily skewed toward shorter-term results. This encourages higher risk-taking to earn the coveted quarterly and annual bonuses, usually in the tens of millions of dollars, at the expense of longer-term performance. But we're getting ahead of ourselves.

The Glass-Steagall Act has been chipped away until its final demise after sixty-seven years of Act-weakening lobbying, just months before the peak in the stock market indices. After its passage in 1933, it went largely unaffected until the 1980s, when the former director of J. P. Morgan became the chairman of the Federal Reserve Board. Alan Greenspan wasted no time expanding supposed GSA loopholes. It should have been no surprise that in 1990, J. P. Morgan became the first bank to receive permission from the cartel to once again underwrite securities. The history of repeal, which began in earnest in the early 1980s, is a study in turf wars among large banks, small banks, brokerage firms, and insurance companies (in 1956, underwriting insurance was forbidden under the Bank Holding Company Act, an extension of GSA) all vying for a larger slice of the ever-growing, lucrative pie. By the end of 1996, the bull market in stocks had been raging for fourteen years and the cartel, under Greenspan, was now permitting up to 25-percent securities underwriting. That gilded the way for the first outright acquisition of a brokerage firm by a bank in 1997. That summer, Greenspan's old bank was in the hunt along with many of the other banks, brokers, and insurance companies. By the spring of 1998, the largest financial services company in the world was the result of the biggest corporate merger in history. However, the GSA—although severely weakened—was still in place. The lobbying effort was intensified.

The Financial Modernization Act: Now, who could vote against something that would leave the old-fashioned GSA behind and launch the U.S. into the twenty-first century? Just like the Coin Modernization Act, which cheapens U.S. coinage even farther from its base metal components, the Graham-Leach-Bliley Act (GLB) would cheapen sound regulation and launch us back to the instability GSA was fighting. Opponents of repeal gave it ten years before we'd see real trouble. They were close! Another bit of irony was Senator Charles Schumer's bravado that had him saying, "If we don't pass this bill, we could find London or Frankfurt, or, years down the road, Shanghai becoming the financial capital of the world. There are many reasons for this bill, but first and foremost is to ensure that U.S. financial firms remain competitive." Funny, the German Boerse (German stock exchange) is buying the New York Stock Exchange (NYSE) in 2011. The NYSE has mostly been a backdrop for photo ops anyway and has been largely symbolic for years. Opponents to GLB have been vindicated. Some proponents are changing the story and making excuses. Don't forget that the abolishment of the

GSA with the birth of the GLB also brought us the infamous Community Revitalization Act, thanks to Senators Christopher Dodd and Charles Schumer.

The repeal of the GSA not only allowed proven risky behavior to return, but also took away the threat of personal liability lawsuits for the CEOs and board members who are now the foxes in the henhouse. It has been a long time since anyone from a publicly traded firm has served time for a financial crime. It is no longer required, as white-collar financial crimes are largely not prosecuted. Fines are preferred. There is a long list of fines levied against firms and individuals, but they amount to only a couple of days worth of revenue or a very small percentage of net worth. A $200-billion crime might come with a $10-million price tag (if you are caught). Hmmm, I'm not very good at math, but spending $1 to keep $20,000 sounds appealing. Here's a *Forbes* blog entry that summarizes one case:

### Why Isn't Angelo Mozilo In Jail?

The perpetually suntanned founder of Countrywide Credit—Angelo Mozilo—made $521.5 million in compensation from 2000 until 2008. He also coined $140 million in gains from selling his Countrywide stock between November 2006 and October, 2007, at the very moment he was learning internally that his company was merchandising soon-to-collapse subprime mortgages— what he described as the most "toxic product" he'd ever seen. He called this expectation "a looming disaster" and the company's "poison," according to internal emails. But, he told no one on the outside, not his shareholders, not the regulators, not his board of directors— not even the politicians like Sen. Dodd for whom he had arranged sweetheart deals.

Strangely unfair, then, that Mozilo was able to settle with the SEC [Securities and Exchange Commission] by paying only $22.5 million of his own personal money as a fine. The other $46 million plus Mozilo's legal fees actually will be paid by Bank of America and insurance policies taken out by Countrywide.

Why isn't it fraud that he "disregarded his duties to investors by concealing what he saw from inside the executive suite," as Robert Khuzami, the hardnosed head of the SEC Enforcement Division put it?

It's the classic "robbery" of white collar executives. They profit hugely themselves, and agree to pay a record fine because it isn't their own money largely that's being coughed up.

Merrill Lynch and therefore Bank of America—which owns Merrill Lynch—owns Countrywide, and has had to face the writeoffs Mozilo hid from view. Let's hope [Bank of America] hires a roughneck litigator and goes after the fraudster for more civil penalties.

No wonder ordinary Americans are in a bloody rage at the enrichment of these bankers—without a jail sentence—when they have paid the price for not knowing their shares were about to be worth next to nothing.[92]

This fine represents 3.3 percent of Mozilo's estimated net worth of $600 million. The terms of the settlement allow him to avoid acknowledging any wrongdoing and further prosecution.

The GLB Act and others have also opened the road to

proprietary trading desks (prop trading) that create volatility with very opaque and quasi-illegal activity in the financial markets. These prop desks make the sponsoring bank billions of dollars. Many brag about having entire quarters or even years without a losing trade. Yet clients of these same firms are left with average or below-average results. Could it be that the clients are advised to "buy" what the prop desk is selling (at a profit) and sell what the prop desk will be running up next, therefore creating enough volume to meet the liquidity needs of the prop desk? No, certainly not; there are laws against that, right? Isn't that what the "self-regulating" Securities and Exchange Commission was created for?

## Bernie Madoff Was Never Caught

The SEC was created in the wake of the crash of '29, as well, to protect the small investor. This Self-Regulating Organization (SRO) is supposed to make the financial markets safe for all to play fair at capitalism. It is the place where the bottom 20 percent of law school graduates lurk. By their own admission, most of the SEC's time is spent watching unmentionable things on the Internet. Because they are attorneys, most have little to no understanding of the financial markets or the increasingly complex products that are manufactured and sold. When the SEC conducts an inquiry, most of the time is spent having industry professionals educate it on how the financial world works. Its agents are woefully inadequate and are ill-equipped to face the complexity of the modern-day financial shell game. When the outcome of a case is steered and influenced by a big bankster, the lapdog SEC attorney complies. The result? A multimillion dollar offer by that investment bank's law firm, drafting the attorney into the big leagues. You can't even make this stuff up! Records show that the SEC knew about Bernie Madoff as far back as 1992. It is widely known that a private citizen outlined the entire case against Madoff and submitted it to the SEC several times, over many years, with updates and mountains of evidence. Nothing happened.

When the rest of the world found out about the monster Madoff, it was because he turned himself in. Decades of fraud, tens of billions of dollars from around the world lost, homicides, suicides, and ruined families were all on the head of the clueless SRO called the Securities and Exchange Commission. There are other con artists like Madoff that the SEC ignored as well. They aren't worth the wasted paper to write about. It is sufficient to note, however, that many were able to escape prosecution for a significant time because of their own lobbying efforts and an SEC that was not willing to exert itself on the most obvious and blatant fraudsters. Oh, they are good at walking into a brokerage office to conduct an "audit" and slap wrists for not having the appropriate files archived—but usually only after their target explains to them the difference between an exchange-traded fund (ETF) and a leveraged buyout (LBO).

## Never Bet Against the House

Trillions of dollars in losses exist off the balance sheets of financial institutions and the Fed. There has been a massive, unrecognized default partly traceable through Troubled Asset Relief Program

(TARP) funds that went to giant corporations (mostly foreign), ostensibly to strengthen their balance sheets and avoid a global economic collapse.

The clear theme in the markets has always been that if and when market and economic conditions warrant, existing legislation is bent, broken, altered, changed, or abolished (roughly in that order) to suit the needs of the cartel. Sometimes these things take decades, but the cartel is amazingly patient and skilled at playing chess. Sometimes, a family member from the next generation completes a move initiated by the previous one. As Chris Powell, secretary-treasurer of the Gold Anti-Trust Action Committee, quipped, "There are no markets anymore, just interventions." If you are not a large, cartel-favored institution with inside information, then you are just a speculator, a gambler. The rules can be changed without prior notice, the game rigged, and exogenous forces handily credited with the cause by the mainstream media, whose members themselves are owned by large, market-moving conglomerates with an agenda. All the while, friends of the cartel are placing "sure bets." Never bet against the house.

Think about what *should* be happening to the institutions that were complicit in the 2008 financial crisis and what is actually happening to them (besides the world-record bonuses in the tens of billions they are paying themselves). Now you get it! The best years as a "too-big-to-jail" institution come after the taxpayer-sponsored bailouts. But wait; doesn't all the taxpayer money go to pay the interest on the dollars borrowed into existence and the subsequent debt? Yes, and the recipient of those dollars, the cartel, lends out billions of that money from the Federal Reserve's emergency lending facility.

Furthermore, these behemoths benefit from a low interest-rate environment created by the cartel's purchasing of Treasury securities. Wouldn't you like to borrow money from the public at a low rate, loan it back at a high rate, and engage in the riskiest of investment behaviors knowing that you get to keep the profits and recover all your losses? You would have no worries about bad investment decisions, losing money, or suffering adverse consequences. The inconvenience of being forced to fly to DC in your corporate jet to participate in a mock inquisition before a declawed subcommittee of set-for-life members of Congress and senators—perhaps on C-SPAN—would be your only consequence. These are the very attorneys who accepted hundreds of millions of dollars in campaign contributions from your ilk, who would not dare embarrass you and are quite uncomfortable with this necessary show as well. The same can't-do elected cabal who will persecute a sports star or incompetent government appointee for major-league missteps live on C-SPAN will surely keep the people diverted from your methods, all the while allowing you to replenish your personal coffers with the fiat that is confiscated from a skillfully entertained public. Right now, that cartel is in the bending-and-breaking-of-the-rules mode with changing and abolishing those rules yet to come.

## What about Bob?

Bob is a retiree who pays for his bills with the income and gains generated from his investment portfolio. He is prudent with his investments to the point of entering stop-loss orders under all of his investments that allow it. That way, if he's out fishing, crabbing, or hiking and the price of any one of his stocks or options should tumble, it is automatically sold at a small loss or even a profit.

The now-infamous flash crash of May 6, 2010, when the Dow Jones Industrial Average lost over one thousand points in twenty minutes, was most likely caused by the operators of the casino. That's almost a $1-trillion loss in a matter of minutes. To this day, mainstream media reports use much more conservative numbers when discussing this event. It used to be that participating brokerage firms called "market makers" maintained the orderly flow of market orders on the exchanges to make sure all participants received what was known as "best execution." Fast forward to 2005, when computer black boxes using top-secret algorithms were allowed to start trading in the markets. These are different from the computer trading blamed for the crash of 1987. These algos don't *facilitate* market activity; they *are* the market activity—up to 70 percent of market activity, by some estimates. This is known as High-Frequency Trading (HFT) and will actually flash large orders (this is a form of frontrunning, is illegal, and is not being prosecuted) on an exchange and then quickly cancel them. This is done in the name of price discovery, market transparency, and provision of liquidity. In reality, these high-speed traders have their super computers co-located with the computers of the exchanges they trade on. Forget the day trading of the nineties; these market wizards are able to trade in millionths of a second and may only hold a stock for a fraction of a minute. Far from providing transparency, liquidity, and orderly markets, these black boxes create volatility, then exploit that volatility by stepping in front of legitimate trades and siphoning hundreds of millions of dollars using nonpublic data. It is widely believed that on May 6, 2010, these algos were caught in a negative feedback loop and started committing fratricide at an alarming rate.

One result was that investors like Bob had every one of their stop-loss orders triggered. Good. Right. Did everything work as it was designed to? No, the orders were sold out at significant percentages below the level they were supposed to be. The exchanges were officially queried on this matter, and they let the trades stand as they were executed, causing tens of thousands of dollars in losses in Bob's retirement account. To make things worse, the NYSE later stepped in and drew a line. Below that line, trades were cancelled. This had never happened before in the history of the stock market. Many of Bob's trades no longer show in the market's time-and-sales price history, but not one dime was returned to him. Why would an individual investor have confidence in an exchange that lets the "too-big-to-jails" play by a different set of rules than the one other investors must abide by?

## The "D" Word

The derivatives bubble dwarfs all other financial bubbles before it...and then some. The notional value of the derivative exposure in the world's markets is many, many times the countries of the world's combined gross domestic product *plus* the total value of all the world's real estate assets. The derivative market is the biggest casino of them all, a real house of cards. Many estimates are in the $600–$700-trillion range; one is a quadrillion dollars. After World War II, wars have been fought in third-world countries. After all, what self-respecting nation wants all that mess on its soil, all that ruined real estate and destroyed landmarks? Now, those countries fight their battles in the financial markets using derivatives. Warren Buffett, the billionaire sage of Omaha, Nebraska, called them "financial weapons of mass destruction."

So, what are they? The *Economic Collapse* blog (www.the economiccollapseblog.com) has the following to say in an entry entitled, "Derivatives: The Quadrillion Dollar Financial Casino Completely Dominated by the Big International Banks":

> If you took an opinion poll and asked Americans what they considered the biggest threat to the world economy to be, how many of them do you think would give "derivatives" as an answer? But the truth is that derivatives were at the heart of the financial crisis of 2007 and 2008, and whenever the next financial crisis happens, derivatives will undoubtedly play a huge role once again. So exactly what are "derivatives"? Well, derivatives are basically financial instruments whose value depends upon or is derived from the price of something else. A derivative has no underlying value of its own. It is essentially a side bet. Today, the world financial system has been turned into a giant casino where bets are made on just about anything you can possibly imagine, and the major Wall Street banks make a ton of money from it. The system is largely unregulated (the new "Wall Street reform" law will only change this slightly) and it is totally dominated by the big international banks.
>
> Nobody knows for certain how large the worldwide derivatives market is, but most estimates usually put the notional value of the worldwide derivatives market some-

where over a quadrillion dollars. If that is accurate, that means that the worldwide derivatives market is twenty times larger than the GDP of the entire world. It is hard to even conceive of 1,000,000,000,000,000 dollars.

Counting at one dollar per second, it would take you 32 million years to count to one quadrillion.

So who controls this unbelievably gigantic financial casino?

Would it surprise you to learn that it is the big international banks that control it?

*The New York Times* [published an article December 12, 2010] entitled "A Secretive Banking Elite Rules Trading in Derivatives." Shockingly, the most important newspaper in the United States has exposed the steel-fisted control that the big Wall Street banks exert over the trading of derivatives. Just consider the following excerpt:

> *On the third Wednesday of every month, the nine members of an elite Wall Street society gather in Midtown Manhattan.*
>
> *The men share a common goal: to protect the interests of big banks in the vast market for derivatives, one of the most profitable—and controversial—fields in finance. They also share a common secret: The details of their meetings, even their identities, have been strictly confidential.*

Does that sound shady or what?

In fact, it wouldn't be stretching things to say that these meetings sound very much like a "conspiracy."

The *New York Times* even named several of the Wall Street banks involved: JPMorgan Chase, Goldman Sachs, Morgan Stanley, Bank of America and Citigroup.

Why does it seem like all financial roads eventually lead back to these monolithic financial institutions?

As the article in the *NY Times* noted:

> *"The revenue these dealers make on derivatives is very large and so the incentive they have to protect those revenues is extremely large," said Darrell Duffie, a professor at the Graduate School of Business at Stanford University, who studied the derivatives market earlier this year with Federal Reserve researchers. "It will be hard for the dealers to keep their market share if everybody who can prove their creditworthiness is allowed into the clearinghouses. So they are making arguments that others shouldn't be allowed in."*

So why should we be so concerned about all of this?

Well, because the truth is that derivatives could end up crashing the entire global financial system.[93]

Here are some past cases of market manipulation using derivatives:

Salomon Brothers, 1991
Fenchurch, 1993
Piper Jaffray, 1994
Orange County California bankruptcy, 1994

Barings Bank bankruptcy, 1995
Sumitomo, 1995–1996
Asian Contagion, 1997
Avista Energy, 1998
Long Term Capital Management bankruptcy, 1999
Enron bankruptcy, 1998, 2000, and 2001
Arcadia, 2001

James Wesley Rawles, editor of www.SurvivalBlog.com, wrote:

When I do radio interviews or lecture presentations, I'm often asked: "Mister Rawles, what do you see as a likely 'worst case scenario'?" People expect me to say "a full scale nuclear exchange in World War III" or, "a stock market crash," or "a flu pandemic," or "a sudden end to the current real estate bubble." But most of them are surprised when I respond: "Economic collapse triggered by the popping of the derivatives bubble." Many people that are involved in the periphery of the investing world—including most small investors—have never even heard of derivatives. They may have heard of "hedge funds," but they don't understand what they are. Yet in terms of the sheer number of dollars, yen, and euros traded, these investments represent the biggest financial market of all.[94]

A familiar derivative would be a cattle futures contract or a call option on General Electric. However, in their worst form, a derivative is as dangerous as taking out an insurance policy on your neighbor's house and then burning down that house to collect on the "insurance." The speculation on the street is that the banksters are taking their big salaries and even bigger bonuses now because their future, as facts become clearer, will be frightfully uncertain even though unwinding it will take their cooperation. Banks no longer live under the specter of looming failure (like every other private enterprise); they live in a world of crony capitalism, knowing the people will pay. Just look at the rate on some people's credit cards! That kind of usurious lending and stealing from the poor, along with guaranteed government bailouts and free money, continues to replenish their coffers.

## What to Do

This chapter is a scratch at the surface of a very deep and broad subject. There has been no mention of the President's Working Group on Financial Markets, aka the "Plunge Protection Team." There is barely a mention of the banksters' influence and control of politics, their appointments to the highest level positions, and their massive campaign contributions and lobbying efforts. Nothing introduces the strategy behind the open, transparent push toward a one-world currency for ultimate control of the population. There's no explanation of survivor bias and manipulation of components of the stock market indices. Rather than being left to feel angry, discouraged, and hopeless, there is much work to be done.

**First,** make sure you are right with God:

"The Lord is nigh unto them that are of a broken heart; and saveth such as be of a contrite spirit" (Psalm 34:18).

"The sacrifices of God are a broken spirit: a broken and a contrite heart, O God, thou wilt not despise" (Psalm 51:17).

"A bruised reed shall he not break, and smoking flax shall he not quench, till he send forth judgment unto victory" (Matthew 12:20).

**Second,** make sure you are right with those around you:

"If it be possible, as much as lieth in you, live peaceably with all men" (Romans 12:18).

"See that none render evil for evil unto any man; but ever follow that which is good, both among yourselves, and to all men. Rejoice evermore. Pray without ceasing. In every thing give thanks: for this is the will of God in Christ Jesus concerning you. Quench not the Spirit. Despise not prophesyings. Prove all things; hold fast that which is good. Abstain from all appearance of evil. And the very God of peace sanctify you wholly; and I pray God your whole spirit and soul and body be preserved blameless unto the coming of our Lord Jesus Christ" (1 Thessalonians 5:15–23).

**Third,** stay abreast of what's happening in the world.

You can't do this by reading and watching the mainstream media. The website www.survivalblog.com features daily posts on economics and investing. The links there will lead you to other sites and information that you will eventually find part of your routine. Check on the pulse of the economic and geopolitical world and more. Also, Franklin Sanders at www.the-moneychanger.com presents wonderful articles on all sorts of topics as well as a must-read newsletter for a very reasonable price. He is a wise man and will challenge your thinking.

**Fourth,** understand your investments.

Markets go through paper asset cycles and hard asset cycles.

If it hasn't become obvious, we are in a hard asset cycle. The most recent paper asset cycle started in 1982 and ended in 2000. That's when the hard asset cycle started. Just pull up a chart on gold or silver, and you'll see it plainly. These cycles tend to last for around twenty years. Think about what comprised someone's wealth before electricity. If your money is in a bank or in a "market," then it exists in electronic form only. Gerald Celente, founder of the Trends Research Institute, says, "It's not worth the paper it's not printed on!" He may be right. You have nothing tangible. Consider moving it to more tangible forms of wealth.

**Fifth,** tell those around you what you are learning. Discuss it. Most people are just concerned with what's on TV, who will be the first-round draft pick, or how the latest celebrity scandal is playing out. Prepare to be discouraged, but persevere.

## chapter nine

# SATAN'S ECONOMY
## The Inescapable, Predestined Endgame

*By Terry James*

**D**ESPITE THE BLATANT evidence to the contrary, the American administration and mainstream news media seem bent on painting a picture of a U.S. and global recovery from the economic plunge taking place since 2008–2009.

One economist who disagrees with the rosy presentation by these "experts" writes the following:

> More and more economists, policymakers, and investors are becoming ever more certain that the good times are here again.
>
> Not even the crises in Japan, the Middle East, Europe, and China can quell the prevailing mood of resolute complacency.
>
> Apparently, the effects of the global crisis…are long past. However, this couldn't be further from the truth.

The soothsayers are unable to discern cause from effect, artifice from reality, wisdom from folly.

Time will judge today's policymakers and opinion makers. The stark reality is really this: conditions are not getting better; actually, the long-term outlook is becoming darker.

The global financial crisis is not over; [it is] only shifting and morphing into new forms.

An unprecedented mix of factors is playing out at present (geopolitically, socially, economically, and financially).[95]

Like it or not, believe it or not, you and I are being swept along by the tide of human history toward something profoundly ominous. Hourly news accounts, no matter how much they've been doctored to try to present a recovering national and global economic picture, engender fearful concerns about things to come.

*Demonomics: Satan's Economy and Your Future* gives tremendous insights into the causes and effects of the evil shaping and moving America and the world toward a destiny the supposed best minds on the planet can't determine. However, that inability to define the problems, much less find solutions, doesn't stop them from making seemingly wild stabs at trying to channel all of us into a drastically changed economic national and world order. But, are their attempts really wild stabs, or is there method to their madness?

History is replete with attempts to reshape national and even global economic realities. Money equals power and power exerts control upon this fallen planet. Power is the ultimate endgame of all who seek it for themselves.

Henry Kissinger put it this way: "Power is the ultimate aphrodisiac."[96] The declaration can be understood in recalling the most ancient of accounts of an infamous personality seeking the greatest of all power:

> For thou hast said in thine heart, I will ascend into heaven, I will exalt my throne above the stars of God: I will sit also upon the mount of the congregation, in the sides of the north: I will ascend above the heights of the clouds; I will be like the most High. (Isaiah 14:13–14)

Man's determination to do the same—acquire the power to which the angel named Lucifer aspired—hasn't changed since the serpent first told Eve that she and Adam would be like God if they ate from the fruit of the forbidden tree (see Genesis 3:5). Following the serpent's trail of power madness to a later time recorded in the Bible, Nimrod was the would-be one-world-order builder of his day, following the Great Flood of Noah's time. He, like every megalomaniac since, lusted for God-like power.

> And the whole earth was of one language, and of one speech. And it came to pass, as they journeyed from the east, that they found a plain in the land of Shinar; and they dwelt there. And they said one to another, Go to, let us make brick, and burn them throughly. And they had brick for stone, and slime had they for morter. And they said, Go to, let us build us a city and a tower, whose top may reach unto heaven; and let us make us a name, lest we be scattered abroad upon the face of the whole earth. (Genesis 11:1–4)

God had instructed man to go forth across the earth and multiply. These people under Nimrod's leadership, like Lucifer, decided to try to usurp God's authority and power. This generation set up headquarters in Shinar, directly in opposition to the Lord's commandment (see Genesis 9:1). They even determined to build a tower that would reach into the abode of God. Like Lucifer, they wanted to make themselves at least equal with the Creator.

Such is the way of man, fallen since the moment of rebellion in the Garden of Eden. Humankind has been determined to do things that seem right in their own eyes. The sin-cursed mindset will continue until the catastrophic second when God must end the rebellion as He first had to do when He destroyed all but Noah and his family in the worldwide Flood.

We are told this in the following prophecy given by the psalmist:

> Why do the heathen rage, and the people imagine a vain thing? The kings of the earth set themselves, and the rulers take counsel together, against the Lord, and against his anointed, saying, Let us break their bands asunder, and cast away their cords from us. He that sitteth in the heavens shall laugh: the Lord shall have them in derision. Then shall he speak unto them in his wrath, and vex them in his sore displeasure.
>
> Yet have I set my king upon my holy hill of Zion. I will declare the decree: the LORD hath said unto me, Thou art my Son; this day have I begotten thee.
>
> Ask of me, and I shall give thee the heathen for thine

inheritance, and the uttermost parts of the earth for thy possession. Thou shalt break them with a rod of iron; thou shalt dash them in pieces like a potter's vessel.

Be wise now therefore, O ye kings: be instructed, ye judges of the earth. Serve the LORD with fear, and rejoice with trembling. (Psalms 2:1–11)

## History Repeating

The Psalms 2 prophecy is in full sail toward the point at which God will put an end to the power madness of His sin-sick creation called man. The God of heaven will send the Son of Man—Jesus Christ—to intervene catastrophically in the insanity we are witnessing through today's headlines.

Man's lust for power continues to grow; he has not learned the lessons of the past because, as a whole, he regards the Word of God as irrelevant to the governance of the earth. One philosopher of renown put it this way: "He who does not remember history is condemned to repeat it."[97]

The corruption that God saw and condemned in antediluvian times, which caused Him to destroy all upon the earth except eight people, has again reached a dangerous level. Dictators prove the truth of another bit of philosophical wisdom: "All power tends to corrupt, and absolute power corrupts absolutely."[98]

We have only to consider the dictators of most recent times to know that lust for power and love of money are locked together in the tyrannical determination to enslave people around the world. Whether remembering Saddam Hussein and his beastly throat-hold on the Iraqi people, the more western-friendly Hosni Mubarek, or many dictators in between, the one thing they have done is to garner to themselves billions of dollars of personal wealth. Their peoples have had incomes per capita far below the lowest of poverty lines in the United States, while most of the Middle East tyrants, for example, are filthy rich in petrodollars—much of which they have received from America. The pre-Ayatollah Kohmeni and Islamist revolution Shah of Iran, were he still alive, could amply testify that such is the catalyst for fomenting riotous uproar.

Here's what one of the writers of God's Word had to say about this truth:

> But they that will be rich fall into temptation and a snare, and into many foolish and hurtful lusts, which drown men in destruction and perdition. For the love of money is the root of all evil: which while some coveted after, they have erred from the faith, and pierced themselves through with many sorrows. (1 Timothy 6:9–10)

Another of God's men chosen to write His truth further speaks to the fate of those who want riches to give themselves power over others:

> Go to now, ye rich men, weep and howl for your miseries that shall come upon you. Your riches are corrupted, and your garments are motheaten. Your gold and silver is cankered; and the rust of them shall be a witness against you, and shall eat your flesh as it were fire. Ye have heaped

treasure together for the last days. Behold, the hire of the labourers who have reaped down your fields, which is of you kept back by fraud, crieth: and the cries of them which have reaped are entered into the ears of the Lord of sabaoth. Ye have lived in pleasure on the earth, and been wanton; ye have nourished your hearts, as in a day of slaughter. Ye have condemned and killed the just; and he doth not resist you. (James 5:1–6)

## Satan's Chief Weapon

Economy—the love of money, thus power over others—is the chief weapon in Lucifer's arsenal of destructive instrumentalities against mankind. Money buys power, whether it means acquisition of luxuries, sexual gratification, or raw, political power.

And Satan has the ability to distribute the earthly wealth of this riches-loving world. Jesus didn't argue with the devil when he took Him to a mountain top and showed Him all the kingdoms and luxuries of the world, saying "All these things will I give thee, if thou wilt fall down and worship me" (Matthew 4:9). The Lord never corrected Satan, telling him that he had no such power to offer those earthly riches. Instead, Jesus did what the rulers of this world more often than not have *not* been able to do—resist the aphrodisiac that is earthly power. Jesus turned Satan's offer into an opportunity to give mankind the absolute truth from the mind of God: "Then saith Jesus unto him, Get thee hence, Satan: for it is written, Thou shalt worship the Lord thy God, and him only shalt thou serve" (Matthew 4:10).

## A Poisonous Potion

The aphrodisiac that is power (wealth, authority, and control) is as deadly in its long-term effects as it is addictively alluring in its siren call. Every empire down through the annals of history has given testimony of the venomous destructiveness of those who murder and plunder to have ever-increasing power. Wealth is in its very essence the toxin that produces the addiction and that inflicts the devastation upon both the wielders and the victims of earthly power.

The power that is driving the massive economic storm of our time is spawned and perpetuated by the evil inhabiting the unseen places—dimensions beyond the visible. The Bible speaks of this force through the apostle Paul: "For we wrestle not against flesh and blood, but against principalities, against powers, against the rulers of the darkness of this world, against spiritual wickedness in high places" (Ephesians 6:12).

Satan's economy has been behind every upheaval and most all bloodshed throughout history. Some authors who have contributed to this book have provided historical perspective on the wars and revolutions that have wreaked havoc on civilizations of practically every era.

## Present Power Plays

Devilish doings can be sensed working behind the scenes of the raging economic turbulence that began with the collapse of an American financial power center. Economics-minded forecasters great and small watched the stock market bubble build during the days preceding the Lehman Brothers collapse of 2008, speculating wildly what the bubble's burst might bring. That financial aneurysm, they determined, would certainly rupture—and, of course, it did. Governmental insanity created by ultraliberal politicians saw to it that people with champagne tastes and beer drinkers' budgets for years received home loans they didn't have much more than a prayer of ever repaying.

We are now familiar with the terms "Freddie Mac" and "Fannie Mae." We are equally acquainted with names such as Barney Frank, Charles Schumer, and others, who—in the name of "fairness" to those who couldn't afford housing like the more affluent—demanded these be given the loans anyway, despite the fact the recipients didn't have the income or collateral to support that level of debt.

Rather than govern the housing industry responsibly, the elected officials invested with the responsibility to oversee things, in concert with their Wall Street cohorts, foolishly threw caution to the fiscal winds. A banking crisis of unprecedented magnitude was thus created, with the housing bubble rupture setting in motion bank failures and threats of even greater crises.

Calls for massive bailouts to avert what the president of the United States and others in government and media speciously screamed would otherwise be world-rending calamity brought about the most devastating crisis of all. Trillions of dollars were, in effect, created out of thin air by the Federal Reserve Bank to save entities "too big to fail."

The totally irresponsible sleight-of-hand accomplished only the creation of an exploding national debt that most likely can never be repaid. Decisions made by some of the same people who help create the problems strapped on the back of American citizens financial burdens with which generations far into the future will have to deal.

The resulting economic uncertainty deepened an abyss-like recession that more soundly thought-out measures would have surely lessened in severity. Jobs, as we know, are being lost; businesses are closing their doors; deflation or hyperinflation—the experts can't figure which—might collapse the American economy within a near-time frame (which the experts can't predict, either).

The stability of the global economy hangs in the balance, with the other nations and their monetary gurus wondering about the financial fate of the U.S. and its all-important dollar. And, make no mistake: Under present world economic structures, the fate of the American dollar is absolutely critical.

## Devil's Workshop

Idleness, it is said, is the devil's workshop. Satan's economy runs best (to his satisfaction) when people have too much free time on their hands. When not preoccupied with work or other productive endeavors, human beings are often susceptible to acting as pawns for carrying out the mischief Satan and his minions—the powers and principalities in high places named in Ephesians 6:12—stir them to accomplish.

This can be demonstrated as true across the spectrum of human activity. The idle rich have been lambasted throughout the centuries for being up to no good. Literature has scathingly addressed the ne'er-do-well nature of the self-absorbed money class—e.g., F. Scott Fitzgerald's *The Great Gatsby*.

At the other end of the socioeconomic spectrum resides the

welfare class, the poorest among the citizenry. They are in the unbreakable grip of a bureaucratic, enabling government that keeps them locked in a sort of cultural disability.

The two extremes are known in philosophical rhetoric as the haves and have-nots. The powers that be—both those of the Ephesians 6:12 sort and of the human sort—play one against the other in class warfare that keeps either from ever coming to a meeting of minds.

Socialism is the human attempt to make the haves give their perceived riches to the have-nots. It is the old Marxist ploy that purports to redistribute the wealth—a phrase we heard Barack Hussein Obama use in saying he was in favor of that very thing during his campaign for the presidency of the United States.

America has been moving toward socialism since before Franklin D. Roosevelt's New Deal and Social Security ideas were implemented. While taking, through taxation, from those who are blessed to have jobs and giving to those who don't have jobs assures that everyone is taken care of to a degree, the process over time cripples, then destroys, incentive to work. It ultimately brings down entire nations.

This is proved by examining the Great Society and War on Poverty of Lyndon B. Johnson's watch as president. Even though trillions of dollars have been poured into those prodigious tax-funded outlays, the number of welfare entitlements the political process has produced has continued to grow. The needs of the have-nots have grown exponentially despite the trillions in outlay, and have brought America to her knees, economically.

In this sense, the largesse—whether well-meaning or otherwise—has enslaved not only the poorest of people within the welfare gulag, but has put in bondage every productive, wage-earning worker in America by seeing to it that future generations are yoked with debt so heavy it can never be paid off.

As of this writing, the national debt is at around $14.4 trillion, and it is growing by billions with each day that passes.

The army of welfare recipients, for the most part, exists unproductively from day to day, awaiting their next government stipend. Much of the youth within this vast cultural morass grow up with their thoughts turned toward crime. The gangs have, in many cases, become the only home life these young people have ever known.

Community organizer types are the beneficiaries of this class warfare, pitting the poorest Americans against those who earn the money to provide the welfare entitlement funding. These organizers stir within the masses of the nonworking classes for votes to achieve power within the American political process.

Now this nation, like most of Europe, has reached the point that providing the same level of such socialistic entitlement can no longer be done. America has gone from being the greatest lender nation ever to exist to possibly, within a short time, being the most indebted nation on the planet.

Not only can welfare and other social programs no longer be supported by government at the same level as they have been to this point; the same is true for the government workers of America, both federal and state. Remember the rage and protests when the governor of Wisconsin announced cuts in state funding? The government workers—stirred into a frenzy by government union organizers and joined by people who looked to be old hippies of the sixties—brought their wrath and destructive ways to bear at the state's capital. An estimated $7 million in damage was done during the course of their "rallies."

## You Ain't Seen Nothing Yet

What we have been witnessing is really the first of the storm fronts to come, economically speaking. A time is coming when the announcement will have to be made that the entitlement programs are being cut.

At that time, depending upon the depth of the cuts that have to be made, there could erupt such rage within those who have for generations received their sustenance without having to work for it that it might become necessary to institute martial law. This is a possible eventuality of which every American must be aware.

The writers of *Demonomics: Satan's Economy and Your Future* have laid out the almost-certain financial calamity awaiting America and the world. Hyperinflation could, overnight, bring about draconian cuts to social entitlements and cause the protest tsunami just mentioned.

This is the sort of tumult that the prince of the power of the air delights in—and I'm not speaking of the head of the Federal Communications Commission. Satan has things boiling all over the world. His chief device for fomenting the violent rage has the slavish love of money at its core.

Greece, Spain, Portugal, Ireland, and other European nations experienced meltdowns because of the turmoil created by mankind's love for money and power. The socialistic give-aways that purchased for the politicians of Europe their positions and sustained them in their seats of authority and control brought European Union members to the brink of insolvency.

The violent demonstrations by those with their "entitlements" cut by the austerity measures threatened anarchy throughout those nations. Like the too-big-to-fail cries applied to the

U.S. financial institutions in crisis, the EU failures could not be allowed to happen. The result is a growing bubble of artificially pumped-up money supply. It is a bubble that must and will burst at some point.

## Middle East Madness

No place on earth is Satan's economic mischief more evident than in the Middle East. While the Western world erupted and boiled over in monetary mayhem, luciferic instigation was afoot in the countries surrounding the central nation of Bible prophecy.

As if on cue, the storm that would affect the Western economies as drastically as the banking and national fiscal failures of America and Europe, the Middle East as well as North Africa were suddenly on fire.

The following is an up-to-date as possible timeline of events outlining the incendiary revolution that has engulfed the region—much of which is home to Israel's enemies. Monetary concerns were the kindling for igniting the fires that continue to spontaneously combust. Many, including this writer, believe the rage is fomented by militant Islamists, most likely those within the Muslim Brotherhood.

- December 17, 2010—Mohamed Bouazizi sets fire to himself in the central Tunisian town of Sidi Bouzid to protest police confiscation of his vegetable cart. His act leads to local demonstrations in support.
- December 18, 2010—Protests begin in Tunisia. Support for protests swells until President Zine el-Abidine Ben

Ali steps down from the presidency and flees the country on January 14, 2011.

- December 29, 2010—Police clash with protesters in Algeria. Widespread protests, demonstrations, and riots rock Algeria from January 3 to January 10. This unrest occurs in nearly all of the cities and towns of this country.
- January 13–16, 2011—Protests are held in Libya.
- January 14, 2011—Protests in major cities in Jordan prompt the government to postpone a rise in fuel prices.
- January 17, 2011—Small protest in Oman is staged to demand better pay and lower costs of living.
- January 18—Sporadic protests break out across Yemen from January 18 to January 20 over the government's proposal to modify the constitution. Riots break out in Aden, leading to conflicts between soldiers and protesters.
- January 18–20, 2011—Protests erupt in Aden, Yemen, over President Ali Abdullah Saleh's efforts to establish himself as president for life.
- January 20, 2011—Protests break out in Ta'izz, Yemen, over President Ali Abdullah Saleh's request for a constitutional amendment allowing him to serve for life. Peaceful protests about housing conditions are staged in Algeria.
- January 22, 2011—A small march of about three hundred people in Algiers, Algeria, is violently broken up by police.
- January 24, 2011—The Libyan government blocks access to www.youtube.com.

- In Khemis El Khechna, Algeria, five hundred people protest housing and living conditions. In Tizi Ouzou, Algeria, parents stage a sit-in protest to demand the release of their children who were arrested earlier in the month.
- January 25, 2011—Like the protests in Tunisia, the protests in Egypt seem to grow and become more intense. By January 28, a government-imposed curfew is widely ignored by protesting Egyptians.
- January 26, 2011—Protests erupt in Jordan and continue until February.
- January 27, 2011—Protests are staged in Yemen.
- January 30, 2011—Protests are held in Khartoum, Sudan. After decades of civil war, Sudan is in the middle of dividing itself into two nations.
- February 4, 2011—In Bahrain, protesters gather in front of the Egyptian embassy in Manama.
- In Jordan, King Abdullah meets with the Muslim Brotherhood. Protesters assemble in front of the Egyptian embassy.
- February 8, 2011—Algerian university students announce an indefinite strike. Some professional paramedics also call for an indefinite strike. Youths in Sidi Amar near Annaba demonstrate to demand jobs.
- February 11, 2011—Protests in Yemen turn violent as those celebrating Mubarak's ouster clash with pro-government civilians. Hosni Mubarak resigns as president of Egypt after ruling for twenty-nine years. Protests in Yemen become violent as pro-government protesters and police clash with anti-government protesters.

- February 12, 2011—Some protests are held in major Iraqi cities. Police and pro-government supporters clash with anti-government protesters in Yemen. Protests in Algeria are energized by the resignation of Egyptian president Hosni Mubarak. Police block entrances to Algiers.
- February 14, 2011—Protests in Bahrain turn violent as police use tear gas and rubber bullets on protesters. The prime minister of the Palestinian Authority, Salam Fayyad, and his cabinet resign. President Mahmoud Abbas tasks Fayyad with forming a new government. Protests in Iran turn violent. Police use tear gas and paint balls to disperse the crowds. Clashes occur between government supporters and anti-government protesters in Yemen. Algerian youths protest over unemployment in Akbou; about thirty are hurt in clashes with the police.
- February 15, 2011—Protests in Libya turn violent as protesters clash with police. Violence continues to escalate. Security forces open fire on protesters.
- February 19, 2011—Anti-government protestors clashed with security forces in Djibouti. Violent protests in Yemen continue to escalate. In Libya, helicopters fire into crowds to disperse protesters. Violence and combat are breaking out across the country.
- February 21, 2011—Chaos and confusion in Libya continue as reports surface of the navy shelling towns and the army fighting amongst itself, as well as of rumors that Qaddafi has fled to Venezuela. Protests in Iraqi Kurdistan turn violent. Libya shuts down Internet communication.

- February 22, 2011—In Libya, Qaddafi appears on television to denounce rumors he has fled the country. Former British Foreign Minister David Owen calls for a no-fly zone over Libya. Qaddafi appears on television in the evening to announce that he will fight anti-government forces. In Bahrain, a funeral for a slain protester takes place at the same time pro-monarchy demonstrators are marching in other parts of the city.

- February 23, 2011—In Libya, there are multiple resignations from the government. The Warfalla, the largest of the indigenous tribes, calls on Qaddafi to step down.

- February 25, 2011—Widespread "Day of Rage" protests are held throughout Iraq. Protesters storm government buildings and police respond violently. Jordan sees its largest protest so far. Between six thousand and ten thousand protesters assemble in Amman.

- February 26, 2011—U.S. President Barack Obama calls on Qaddafi to step down as leader of Libya. Sultan Qaboos ibn Sa'id of Oman announces changes to his cabinet, increases some benefits for students at the Higher College of Technology, calls for consumer protection by the government body, and reduces the amount employees must contribute to the Civil Employees Pension Fund.

- February 27, 2011—The UN Council votes to impose sanctions on Libya. Violent and widespread clashes continue in the civil war.

- February 28, 2011—Ships from the U.S. Navy appear off the coast of Libya. British Prime Minister David

Cameron calls for a no-fly zone over Libya. The U.S. freezes Libyan assets.

- March 1, 2011—The National Unity Rally continues the protests in Bahrain. Tens of thousands participate. A pro-government rally is held in Muscat, Oman. Sporadic protests continue in Jordan.
- March 1–30, 2011—Civil war rages in Libya.
- March 4, 2011—The Yemeni military uses rockets and artillery against anti-government protesters. Police and security forces fill the streets of Djibouti to successfully prevent planned protests.
- March 5, 2011—In the prior week, up to thirteen members of the Yemeni parliament have resigned to protest of the violence used against anti-government protesters. Oil workers in Haima, Oman, stage a sit-in to demand better wages and more government investment in the area.
- March 7, 2011—Sultan Qaboos ibn Sa'id of Oman issues eight royal decrees. He abolishes the Ministry of National Economy and forms a committee to audit the state's finances.
- March 8, 2011—Some army troops join the anti-government protesters in Yemen. Widespread violence continues. Violence in Yemen escalates. On March 18, President Ali Abdullah Saleh declares a state of emergency.
- March 9, 2011—The European Parliament urges all European nations to recognize the National Interim Council as the government of Libya.
- March 12, 2011—Thousands of Syrian Kurds protest in Syria.

- March 13, 2011—Riot police use tear gas and rubber bullets against protesters in the financial district of Bahrain. Riot police also attack protesters at Pearl Roundabout.
- March 14, 2011—The Gulf Cooperation Council (GCC) (Bahrain, Saudi Arabia, Kuwait, Oman, Qatar, and the United Arab Emirates) agrees to send troops into Bahrain to guard oil and gas installations and financial institutions. Troops begin to arrive. The crown prince holds talks with the opposition about reform.
- March 15, 2011—Simultaneous demonstrations in major cities across Syria. King Abdullah of Jordan announces the formation of a fifty-three-member committee, which will include government officials and opposition leaders to draft new laws for parliamentary elections and political parties, and sets a three-month deadline for agreement on political reforms. King Hamad of Bahrain declares a three-month state of emergency. Clashes between anti-government protesters and security forces escalate. Britain advises British nationals to leave Bahrain.
- March 16, 2011—GCC forces begin to violently disperse the protesters. The Bahrain Stock Exchange does not open. The UN approves intervention in Libya. A no-fly zone is imposed.
- March 17, 2011—Protesters in Kerbela, Iraq, demonstrate against Saudi-Arabia intervention in Bahrain.
- March 18, 2011—Violence erupts between Syrian protesters and government security forces. Protests are in

multiple cities. Pro-government civilians also clash with anti-government protesters.

- March 20, 2011—Widespread protests in Morocco affect more than sixty cities.
- March 21, 2011—Protests in Daraa, Syria, continue for the fourth day. Protests spread to many cities in Syria.
- March 24, 2011—The Syrian government announces a cut in tax rates and an increase in public-sector salaries. Plans to increase press freedom, create more employment opportunities, and reduce corruption are also announced. The possibility of lifting the emergency law and licensing political parties is raised by a government official.
- March 25, 2011—Widespread violence occurs in Syria as government security forces use deadly force to disrupt the protests. Government buildings are burned and statues destroyed. Reports of protester deaths vary from twenty to dozens. "Day of Rage" protests are organized by Bahraini protesters, but quickly broken up by security forces with tear gas and rubber bullets.
- March 26, 2011—Violent protests in Syria spread across the country.
- March 29, 2011—In Syria, President Bashar al-Assad accepts the resignation of the government. A new government is expected to be formed and announced soon.
- March 30, 2011—Dozens of leaders of countires representing the international community declare in London that Col. Muammar el-Qaddafi should relinquish power in Libya.[99]

## The Endgame

Satan's economy is being shaped before the eyes and ears of all who will pay attention. But, most of the world—even here in America where the free flow of information is unprecedented in history—is paying scant attention to the true nature of unfolding issues and events.

All of this is moving toward a predestined finale, according to God's Word. The grand maestro orchestrating the end-of-days global economic order is none other than the serpent that started it all with his seduction of Eve as recorded in Genesis chapter 3.

The authors of this book have masterfully explained specifically what is going on—how things have and are being manipulated to achieve whatever ending will eventuate. God' prophetic Word will complete your education in demonomics. The One who knows the end from the beginning has omnisciently prepared for you an outline of Satan's blueprint for your future.

Satan is working behind the scenes with supernatural cunning to create chaos within the economies of the world. His intention is to bring about panic at a level that will incite universal demand for new world financial order. That new economic global order can't be achieved as long as sovereign national monetary systems exist.

Here is Satan's endgame in a scriptural nutshell:

And he causeth all, both small and great, rich and poor, free and bond, to receive a mark in their right hand, or in their foreheads: And that no man might buy or sell, save he that had the mark, or the name of the beast, or the number of his name. Here is wisdom. Let him that hath understanding count the number of the beast: for it is the number of a man; and his number is Six hundred threescore and six. (Revelation 13:16–18)

Somehow, all nations—all peoples—must come under the 666 system of numbers and marks. This will happen because God's Word says so. He cannot lie. It will be a totally different economic regime from any on earth today. But, one can sense that the instrumentalities already exist to implement and administrate such a regime. Satellites, computers, and electronic/biological chip devices come to mind, for starters.

The fiat money of the Antichrist will almost certainly be electronic in nature—an electronic funds transfer (EFT) system along the lines of the Special Drawing Rights (SDR) utilized in financial institution money exchanges today.

I personally believe it will be a hybrid Internet system in conjunction with EFT that will give Antichrist the tyrannical control after which Satan lusts. He wants to be worshiped; that is his endgame. He will force all within his reach to do so, and he will use control of economy to accomplish that.

Those who wield the power at the top of the present world economic system will never agree easily to give up their authority. Nations won't voluntarily surrender governmental or monetary sovereignty. It will require a crisis of unprecedented magnitude to cause fear sufficient to convince the powers that be to bow the knee to the prophesied Beast described in Revelation 13. My own belief is that it will be the Rapture of the church that will provide that crisis.

## chapter ten

# SEVEN FINANCIAL STRATEGIES

## For Uncertain Economic Times

*By Jerry Robinson*

Aᴍᴇʀɪᴄᴀ ʜᴀs ᴇɴᴏʀᴍᴏᴜs financial problems that are not going away any time soon. These problems require solutions, yet, unfortunately, our nation's leaders appear unwilling to take the political risks necessary to confront them. It is safe to assume these financial problems will have to inflict massive amounts of pain before America's politicians will lift a finger in an effort to solve them. So, if you think that Washington will solve any of these crises before they begin to impact you and your community, you are sadly mistaken. As Winston Churchill once quipped: "You can always count on *Americans* to do the right thing—after they've tried everything else."

After reading the preceding chapters, the phrase "ignorance is bliss" should take on an entirely new meaning in your mind. By now, you know the brutal truth. But understanding the problem is just the first step. *The next step is to prepare.* After all, what good is it to see the writing on the wall if it does not stir us to take action?

In the book of Proverbs, wise King Solomon wrote: "A prudent man foreseeth the evil, and hideth himself: but the simple pass on, and are punished" (Proverb 22:3). My hope, through this brief chapter, is that you will heed the obvious signs of this nation's financial meltdown by becoming proactive. The time for debate is over. Now is the time for preparation.

Every day, our financial organization, MakersGroup Financial LLC (www.makersgroupfinancial.com), helps educate people just like you through our daily news organization, www.FTMDaily. com; our weekly radio program, *Follow the Money Weekly;* our monthly educational webinars; and our quarterly investment newsletter, *Follow the Money Quarterly.* Because we speak directly to the economic times, we get a lot of questions. The most common one I receive after lecturing on the topic of America's economic crisis is: "What should I be doing with my money right now?" Since I do not believe in a one-size-fits-all approach to personal finances, I am always hesitant to hand out specific advice to someone I have just met. However, I do believe that nearly everyone can benefit from considering a handful of common-sense financial strategies. *Of course, you should always consult with a professional financial advisor prior to making financial decisions.*

In this chapter, I am going to give you *seven powerful financial strategies* we use every day here at our organization. I believe these will help you weather the current financial storm and especially the greater one to come. These strategies are certainly not all you will need for the days ahead, but they are a good start in the right direction.

## Seven Strategies for Overcoming Economic Adversity

Today, many people have no financial game plan and, if they do have one, it is often backwards. Some may have a few investments, but little in liquid savings. Others may have some savings and investments, but they are woefully underinsured for a personal crisis. Others have investments that are poorly diversified. Furthermore, most people are dependent upon only one stream of income and are, therefore, financially vulnerable in the event of a sudden job loss.

If any of the above describes you, take heart. It is not too late to make a positive change for your financial future. Regardless of your age or economic situation, you still have time to set financial goals. In fact, setting financial goals is one of the most important steps you can take when it comes to wisely stewarding the money entrusted to you. This brings us to our first financial strategy.

### FINANCIAL STRATEGY #1: Commit Yourself to Financial Education

> "My people are destroyed for lack of knowledge."
>
> HOSEA 4:6

For far too long, Americans have been economically illiterate. This is not acceptable if we desire to be wise stewards of the finances and resources that God has placed in our hands. As Americans, each of us lives at a higher standard than does much of the world outside our nation's borders. However, this blessing comes with responsibility. The Bible says that those to whom much is given, much is required (see Luke 12:48). The journey towards becoming good overseers of our God-given resources begins with information. There is much you can do to inform yourself and others.

*First, dedicate yourself to economic awareness.*

With the unfolding of the U.S. financial crisis, the importance of understanding basic economics has been forced upon average Americans. Every day, we hear words like "interest rates," "the Fed," and "the euro," just to mention a few. The truth is that the basic laws of economics are important to every American because they affect every American. By choosing to buy and read this book, you have demonstrated concern about the direction of this nation's economy. You have also shown that you are dedicated to good financial stewardship. But don't stop here. Commit to making yourself aware, and then do all you can to safeguard your financial future. Remember, very few people are really looking out for you in this world. No one cares about your financial future as much as you do.

*Second, keep current with financial news both here and abroad.*

Life in the information age is interesting. On one hand, it means we have information literally at our fingertips. But it also means we must be careful in deciding whom we choose to listen to and what we believe. The more you read about money, the more you will discover that a substantial amount of economic news is not worth the paper it is printed on. Much of the financial press contains contradictory advice on money and investing and can confuse more than it helps. However, I do recommend a few news sources. The *Wall Street Journal* is still one of the best sources for getting solid reporting on financial news and global economic issues. Another U.S. publication I recommend is *Investor's Business Daily*. As far as international news sources, I highly endorse the *Financial Times*. It is based in London and provides a European perspective of the global economy. I also suggest visiting our website, www.FTMDaily.com, which is committed to publishing important economic trends and forecasts you and your family can use to make wise decisions.

### Third, take an economics or money management course.

Check with your local community college for a beginner's course on economics or money management. This is such an important step because most of us have never learned how money really works. I believe every high school student should have to pass an economic and money-management test before obtaining a diploma. It is simply amazing how little real-world training goes on in most of our public schools. Many high school graduates don't even know how to make a basic budget or how to write a check! You can also find helpful financial and investing articles for beginners online at www.investopedia.com.

### Fourth, study personal finance books.

An abundance of books have been written to help individuals become better money managers. Many offer great insights and are worth reading. However, the best recommendation I can make is to study what the Bible says about money management. Before you say that studying about money in the Bible is "unspiritual," consider that **the Bible has more than 2,350 verses directly dealing with money and possessions.** *That's around twice the number of verses than the Bible contains on faith, prayer, and love combined!* If this topic is that important to God, then shouldn't it be important to us? Find out what God's Word has to say about money. It will revolutionize your views and anchor you with wisdom in times of volatility.

*Fifth, share what you have learned with others.*

One of the most important things you can do for others is share the truth about what is really happening in our economy so they can make wise financial decisions, too. Now that your eyes have been opened, tell those you love and care about what you have learned. Pass this book on to them.

## ACTION STEP #1

The first action step in creating your financial game plan is to commit to educating yourself about money, economics, and personal finance.

## FINANCIAL STRATEGY #2: Create a Charitable Giving Plan

"But this I say, He which soweth sparingly
shall reap also sparingly; and he which soweth
bountifully shall reap also bountifully.
Every man according as he purposeth in his heart,
so let him give; not grudgingly, or of necessity:
for God loveth a cheerful giver."

2 CORINTHIANS 9:6, 7

The first financial strategy mentioned above involves the mind. But this second financial strategy relates to the heart. Money is a funny thing. While it is completely amoral in and of itself, it has the unusual power of being able to destroy individuals. As highlighted throughout the preceding chapters, the love of money is strongly warned against in Scripture, particularly in 1 Timothy 6:10, which makes the profound statement that the root of all evil is the love of money. Money can make our lives very comfortable, but it can also darken our hearts and cause us to rely less and less upon our faith. For this reason, the second strategy in creating your financial game plan must be to determine how much money you are going to give away. If that sounds backwards, it is because our culture has infiltrated and poisoned our minds to the point that we have forgotten that the money we earn, save, and invest is not ours in the first place. It has been said that "Christians show who they are by what they do with what they have." That is true because "where your treasure is, there will your heart be also" (Matthew 6:21). All of us have been entrusted with what we have. Our first priority is to properly recognize this truth by taking the time to decide how we will go about the joyful task of giving. Unfortunately, many people skip this most important step. They justify it by promising themselves that they will come back to it later when they actually have some money to give. But this logic is usually flawed, for if they won't give a small gift, why would they ever give a large one? This is a crucial measure, one that will determine the direction you will head, and the blessings that will await you in the future.

What exactly do I mean by creating a charitable giving plan? If you are an investor, you know that before buying, it is wise to do your own due diligence. That is, you want to investigate before you act to determine whether the investment is a good idea. Some people may spend days, even weeks, sizing up an opportunity before investing. Why do they do this? Because they want to maximize their returns and avoid losses. I believe we should do something similar when it comes to charitable giving. As you build your financial game plan, set financial goals for yourself. This includes dreaming about your financial future and what you want it to look like. Why not spend some time "dreaming" about your future giving as well? It's easy to think: "Wouldn't it be nice if I made $250,000 per year?" or "I can't wait until I finally save $1 million and then live off of the interest." But what if our dreams also included things like: "I hope that I can make a difference with the money I am going to make through my wise investments"? Or "My goal is to give more this year than I gave last year—for the rest of my life"?

*How* our lives would be different if, instead of seeking to consume all of our future wealth, we would look for ways to help others with it! I know what you are thinking: If you give away all of your money, how can you enjoy any of it? Rest assured, I am not talking about giving away all of your money—just a percentage. This percentage can, and should, be defined in advance. Perhaps it is 10–15 percent, or possibly even more. Regardless, the specific percentage is between you and God. It is no one's decision but your own.

One of the greatest hallmarks of true Christianity is generosity. The Bible tells us that genuine happiness is found when we give. When we give, we are simply imitating God, the biggest giver of them all. As the Scripture says, "For God so loved the world, that he gave his only begotten Son" (John 3:16).

During a time of lack, it can be very tempting to slow giving to the work of the gospel. This is a dangerous practice, because the Bible tells us that God watches how we use the money He places in our lives as a way to examine our hearts. The money that has entered your life is a test, pure and simple. We know God owns everything, including the money sitting in your bank account. He is not a tyrant who demands all of your money. On the contrary, He is a loving Father who knows what's best for His children. He knows that the greatest joy in the world is found in giving of ourselves and our resources for His divine purposes.

ACTION STEP #2

Before moving on to the next strategy, take some time to "dream" up a charitable giving plan and then take steps to put it into action.

## Financial Strategy #3: Begin a Systematic Savings Plan

"Go to the ant, thou sluggard; consider her ways,
and be wise: which having no guide, overseer,
or ruler, provideth her meat in the summer,
and gathereth her food in the harvest."

Proverbs 6:6–8

Let's face it: Americans are not good savers. Apparently, we think we don't need to worry about having a "rainy day" fund because we assume the sun will always shine. Nothing could be farther from the truth. *Saving money is a biblical principle that helps insulate us from peril during times of economic uncertainty.*

When we talk about saving money, we are really talking about *planning*. In order to plan, you have to get serious about your money. You have to take control of what you have, and you have to want to save. But planning to save money is just the first step. Someone accurately once said: "You can be on the right track, but if you just sit there, you may get run over."

Being on the right track by planning to save money is good, but if it just remains a plan that never gets put into action, it will never bear fruit. However, once we do begin to work our plan by saving money, we often find distractions along the way. According to the adage that "the road to success is marked with many tempting parking spaces," something will always come up to compete with your plan to save. *This is why I recommend automating your savings plan.* This is easily accomplished now with direct deposit and automatic debiting of specified percentages of your paycheck into your savings account.

Many may already have a systematic savings program. For others, saving money on a regular basis may be a difficult habit to form. This is especially true if it seems that you are barely getting by right now without saving any money. If this describes you, then creating a systematic savings program is one of the most important financial steps for you to take right now.

Several years ago, when I first started trying to save a percentage of my income, I became very easily discouraged. Something would come up every month to prevent me from putting money back. It was not until I learned about something I now call the "Profit Principle" that I began to take saving money very seriously. One day while reading through the book of Proverbs, one verse literally jumped off the page at me: "In all labour there is profit: but the talk of the lips tendeth only to penury" (Proverbs 14:23).

The word that caught my attention was the word "profit." I knew the definition of "profit" was essentially "the amount of income left over after expenses." It was at that moment that I discovered the Profit Principle.

The Profit Principle simply says this: An individual's profit from work is equivalent to the amount of money saved. Simply put, your savings is the profit of your labor.

In truth, each month that I did not save money from my paycheck was a month when I did not earn a profit! Suddenly, I recognized that I was going to work every day for zero profit! Today, large corporations operate their businesses for maximum profit. Additionally, small business owners are dependent upon their profits to survive and thrive. So why should you view your job any differently? *Would you ever agree to work at a job without earning a profit?* Of course not! Yet, millions of Americans work for no profit because they save nothing. I should know, because I used to be one of them!

To make matters worse, many Americans not only earn zero profit from their labor because they do not save; they actually agree to *give away* all of their profits to credit card companies and other corporations! How is this not a form of voluntary slavery?

This financial strategy will help you take back the most basic of your fundamental financial rights—*your right to earn a profit from your labor.* It is biblical, and it makes common sense that you should have control of the profits that are created as a result of your hard work.

After I discovered the Profit Principle, I began to view the money coming into my life very differently. I was not so eager to spend my paycheck on frivolous things or things that I "just had to have." I began to prioritize and cut the "fat" from my monthly budget. Things that used to be important to me, such as maintaining a particular image or keeping up with the Joneses, suddenly faded. (After all, in case no one has told you, the Joneses are **broke**. So why try to keep up with them anyway?)

After you decide it is time to start earning a profit from your labor, your next step is to determine your desired monthly profit rate. You obviously have expenses, so you cannot possibly set your profit rate at 100 percent (although, wouldn't that be nice?). Some of you can set your profit (savings) rate to 10 percent. Others can set their profit rate at 15–20 percent. Many people living in Asian countries, especially in China, have savings rates of over 40 percent!

How much money should you save? I believe the *minimum*

anyone should save is 15 percent of monthly income. **Why 15 percent and not 10 percent, as most financial advisors recommend?** I suggest 15 percent because of the various eroding factors that affect our money. For example, the combined impact of inflation and taxes alone are a good enough reason to save more than 10 percent. These two factors have a tremendous wealth-destroying effect and must be fought aggressively. Those who recommend a 10 percent savings rate may mean well, but that percentage will barely keep your financial head above water over the long run if inflation drifts higher and when, *not if,* tax rates increase.

However, what if you are currently just barely getting by? Try setting your profit rate at 1 percent right now. Then, every month thereafter, you can attempt to raise your profit rate by another percentage point. This will allow you to ease into this strategy without throwing your entire financial game plan into chaos. With this approach, you could realistically have a 10 percent profit rate from your labor by the end of the year.

The important thing is to begin saving money now, and regularly. It's time for you to finally earn a profit from your labor!

---

**ACTION STEP #3**

Determine what you want your profit rate to be and then begin withholding it from your paycheck systematically.

## FINANCIAL STRATEGY #4: Build and Maintain Six Months of Emergency Liquid Savings

"A prudent man foreseeth the evil,
and hideth himself: but the simple pass on,
and are punished."

PROVERBS 22:3

After you decide on your monthly profit (savings) rate, you will have the satisfaction of seeing your savings grow each month. With this financial strategy, you are going to build an emergency pool of liquid savings that is equivalent to six months of your gross income. So, if you earn $3,500 per month, your goal will be to save $21,000 ($3,500/month times six). This money is going to help you in many ways.

Without an emergency fund, you have to rely upon credit, family members, friends, or current investments every time a crisis arises. But this will no longer be necessary (except in rare cases) when you have accumulated a six-month supply of cash.

Additionally, knowing that you have a little extra money in the bank will provide you with priceless peace of mind. This is especially true in our current environment of creeping inflation, corporate layoffs, and high unemployment.

And as you begin to save, you will actually set yourself up to become a savvy investor. This is because good savers make even better investors. Why? Due to something I call the "Risk Relation Principle." That is, the amount of risk someone is willing to take is inversely related to the amount of liquid savings he or she holds. This principle explains why many investors who have little or nothing in savings seek to "hit a home run" with virtually every investment. Because people who do this have no liquid savings, they take excessive—often unnecessary—risks with capital in the hopes of parlaying the little money they do have into something bigger. In essence, they want to make up for their lack of disciplined savings through gambling with investments. This investing approach is usually a sure ticket to the poorhouse!

Furthermore, those who have no liquid savings are often required to tap whatever little money they do have in investments when a calamity arises. This truth became abundantly clear in our most recent financial crisis, when many unemployed Americans were forced to cash in their 401(k)s and IRAs just to pay their mortgages or monthly bills. Others were forced to sell their homes or other investments in order to cover payments that a well-planned emergency fund would have covered. Further, not only did they have to tap into their long-term investments just to cover short-term expenses, but their lack of liquid savings also forced them to cash in their chips when the markets were at a major low. But it's hard to blame them. After all, these underprepared Americans were simply following the financial advice of Wall Street—or even worse, of their human resources department at work. The bad advice goes something like this: "Max out your 401(k), open a traditional IRA, and buy a house, because real estate always goes up in value." Unfortunately, all three of these investment vehicles are designed to be illiquid; they will do little good when you need cold, hard cash quickly.

Finally, there is one rule regarding your six-month pool of emergency savings. You must keep it liquid at all times. This means that it should never be "locked up" in any way. You must always have immediate access to this money, or else it does you no good.

> **ACTION STEP #4**
>
> Flow your profits (savings) into a savings or
> money market account until it reaches an
> amount that is equivalent to six months of your
> gross income, and keep it accessible at all times.

**A quick note:** The first four strategies we've suggested are designed to get your financial house in order. The final three strategies relate exclusively to diversification—namely, diversifying your six-month pool of liquid savings, your investment portfolio, and finally, your income.

Let's now consider the importance of diversifying your savings.

## FINANCIAL STRATEGY #5: Diversify your Savings

> "The silver is mine, and the gold is mine,
> saith the LORD of hosts."
> HAGGAI 2:8

One of the most popular fiscal concepts today is the need for diversification. Unfortunately, most financial advisors only apply this notion to your investments and not to your savings or income. In this financial strategy, I will explain the benefits of keeping your six-month liquid pool of savings diversified.

Once you commit to a 15-percent savings plan, it won't be long before you begin to accumulate a nice sum of money. As we discussed in the last strategy, your initial goal will be to save 50 percent of your annual gross income (or six months of income) through your monthly contributions. Building that reserve of liquid cash will help shield you from the uncertain times that lie ahead. This means that if you earn $30,000 per year, you should build and maintain a minimum of $15,000 in liquid savings *at all times.*

As your savings continue to grow, you will want to begin diversifying the funds in safe places. These funds will need to remain in highly liquid accounts, in case you need to access them quickly. The diversification model I personally like is the following:

- One-third U.S. dollar denominated assets (interest-bearing accounts, CDs, properly structured, cash-value life insurance, etc.)
- One-third hard assets (precious metals, real commodities)
- One-third select, stable foreign currencies (hard currency, CDs, etc.)

## Sample Liquid Cash Savings Allocation

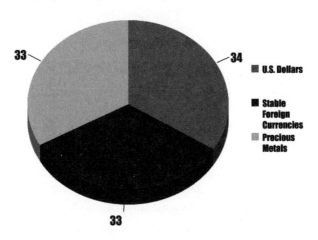

By spreading your liquid savings across a variety of savings vehicles, you will help ensure that your money is not too highly exposed to risk in any one area. And by keeping only one-third of your money in U.S. dollar-denominated assets, you will protect yourself from further declines to the dollar's purchasing power.

**Just as diversifying your money is important, so is keeping it in a safe place.** Just ask anyone who lived during the Great Depression when more than ten thousand banks closed their doors. Many of these institutions did not allow people to take out their funds. Why was that? Well, it's a little-known fact that the banks do not actually have all of your money. This is due to the legal practice of fractional-reserve banking, covered earlier in this book.

I recommend periodically investigating the bank or financial institution that is holding your money. Make sure it is FDIC insured. The FDIC is a government entity that insures the majority of the nation's banks. If your money is on deposit in a FDIC-insured bank, then it is insured up to an amount regulated by the federal government. Currently, this maximum is set at $250,000.

Recently, however, there have been many concerns about the FDIC's ability to handle a major banking crisis. According to the latest reports, the FDIC is responsible for covering $5.4 trillion of qualified bank deposits. How much money does the FDIC have to cover those deposits? Zero. It is actually running an $8 billion deficit. For this reason, consider not keeping any more than the government-set maximum amount in any one bank. *Also, take note that items placed in a bank's safe-deposit box are not considered a deposit account and are, therefore, not FDIC insured.*

In addition, it is a very good idea to investigate the banks where you are currently, or are considering, conducting business. This is especially important, since I believe we are going to witness a large number of bank failures in the not-too-distant future. To check your bank's health, visit www.veribanc.com or www. bankrate.com.

To learn more about foreign currencies, visit www.everbank. com. This site has a large amount of information about all of the popular foreign currencies available to U.S. citizens. To learn more about precious metals like gold and silver, check out our free ninety-minute webinar on precious-metals investing at www. ftmdaily.com.

## ACTION STEP #5

Protect the purchasing power of your six-month pool of liquid savings by diversifying it among a few select areas.

## FINANCIAL STRATEGY #6: Begin a Diversified Investment Portfolio

"Cast thy bread upon the waters:
for thou shalt find it after many days.
Give a portion to seven, and also to eight;
for thou knowest not what evil shall be upon the earth."

ECCLESIASTES 11:1–2

Once you have built up your six-month savings reserve then, *and only then,* it is time to think about "investing." The difference between saving and investing has been lost in today's financial world, which has become dominated by Wall Street banks that need your capital to survive. Therefore, they de-emphasize your need for liquidity and emphasize investing your money with them for as long as possible.

You will want a portion of your investments to be liquid. However, because you have built up your six-month savings reserve, you can more easily invest for the long-term without constantly needing to tap your investments funds in times of an emergency.

When it comes to diversifying your investments, you should seek to spread your funds among *many different asset classes.* Today, the most common retirement plan in America consists of owning a house and having a 401(k) retirement plan. The major problem with these assets, besides being very illiquid, is that they are both completely government-controlled. This is not to say that they don't deserve a place in your financial game plan. Instead, it is to say that they should not be viewed as the "silver bullets" of retirement planning. They certainly are not.

Some people say that diversification is only important for those who do not know how to invest. This is a lie. The truth is that diversification is the ultimate protection against an out-of-control government and federal tax code.

In case no one has told you, earning, saving, and investing in America has become a game. And the rules of the game are found in America's tax code. If you play by the rules, you can do very well in this country. But if you don't play by the rules, you will be punished. Who makes the rules? The federal government. Plus, it can change the rules at any time. That is why smart investors and business owners seek the best tax advisors money can buy.

Since the federal government can change the rules at any time, your only defense is to diversify across a wide variety of asset classes with different tax treatments. This way, if the rules change suddenly, you will not be wiped out.

For example, the tax code currently favors investing in real estate and tax-deferred retirement accounts. However, if the tax code were to change, which it could at any time, then those who have all of their investments in these vehicles could be in for a big surprise.

As you approach investing, look for investments that have favorable tax treatment and provide protection from the inflation we see on the not-too-distant horizon.

The best hedges against inflation are hard assets. These include precious metals, commodities, fine art, and more. Basically, hard assets are tangible assets that you can physically touch and handle. Two of the more exciting areas of hard assets right now are precious metals and agricultural commodities. Here at our organization, we have created an inflation-proof investment philosophy called PACE investing. This is an acronym: P= Precious Metals, A= Agriculture, C=Commodities, E= Energy.

We have been focused on these areas for several years, and the benefits have been immense. Since 2007, I have been urging individuals just like you to consider diversifying their investments into these areas.

What I find interesting about precious metals is their current lack of ownership in America. For example, consider the following chart detailing the breakdown of global liquid wealth.

## Breakdown of Global Liquid Wealth

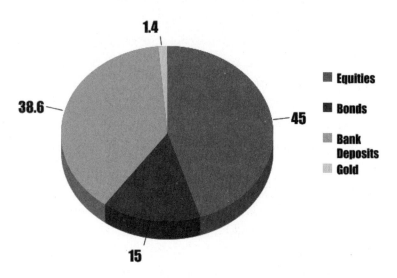

Across the globe, investors now own the largest amount of liquid "paper" wealth in recorded history. Out of all of the liquid assets owned worldwide, gold only makes up a fractional 1.4 percent. According to Anthony Allison from the PFS Group, "If just one or two percent of the world's liquid wealth moved into gold in future years, the price rise would be explosive."

Precious metals are typically scorned by governments that churn out paper (fiat) currencies. Their disdain for precious metals is obvious, as precious metals have historically constrained the overproduction of paper currencies. In today's economy, U.S. dollars are printed at will and devalued as needed. *Regardless of the government's opinion, precious metals such as gold and silver easily outperform in the midst of economic uncertainty.* And if anything is certain, it is that the outlook for the global economy in the coming years is uncertain. **Precious metals always have**

**and always will be the beneficiary of poor monetary policies.** So as America's economy continues to worsen over the coming months and years, I expect more investment dollars to pour into the safe haven of precious metals, thus driving their prices up to very high levels.

Before you invest in gold or silver, or any investment for that matter, always seek advice from a financial professional. Our organization has produced a free, ninety-minute educational webinar on the history and future of precious metals. View it at www.ftmdaily.com.

While I am on the topic of investing, allow me to issue a cautionary note about stock investing in general. Many good men and women who want to get ahead financially come to the stock market with dollar signs in their eyes. They simply want to provide a better future for themselves and their families. Be warned up front: No one—not even the professionals who manage money for a living—knows what the stock market will do. Wall Street is a well-oiled machine in which a novice investor can lose his shirt overnight. Like many, I have made money in the stock market—and I have also lost money. Investing should be approached only after due diligence. Maintain realistic expectations, and don't fall for the hype. *Before investing in anything, consult a trusted financial advisor.*

Like never before, it has become vital to read between the lines of the news coming daily from the American media machine, especially in the business world. The majority of the American media is economically illiterate and pushes "doctored" government numbers for a living. I cannot even begin to tell you how many contradictions I see in the business news on a monthly basis.

If you desire to invest in the markets, do so carefully and after much research. You owe it to yourself and your family to distinguish between fact and fiction in the stock market. Not only will a keen awareness of the economy allow you to protect your current assets, but your future wealth depends on it.

> ACTION STEP #6
>
> Protect your growing investment portfolio by keeping it diversified among a variety of asset classes.

## STRATEGY #7: Diversify Your Income

> "And the LORD hath blessed my master greatly;
> and he is become great: and he hath given him flocks,
> and herds, and silver, and gold, and menservants,
> and maidservants, and camels, and asses."
>
> GENESIS 24:35

Millions of Americans are one paycheck away from foreclosure on their homes. If you lost your job today, would you still have an income a month from now? If not, definitely consider diversifying your income by adding another income stream. Just as you should spread out your savings and investments, I also believe you should diversify your income. Like the old saying goes, "Don't put all of your eggs in one basket." It is my personal belief that everyone should have a minimum of two streams of regular income during the working years, and a minimum of five streams at retirement. Abraham exhibited this quality in that the Bible tells us that he was rich in cattle, slaves, gold, and silver (see Genesis 13:2 and 24:35).

*The nice thing is that you don't need a lot of money to create multiple streams of income.* But you do need some creativity and a willingness to work hard. By diversifying your income through the creation of multiple streams of income, you will be placing a safety net under you and your family in the event of unforeseen circumstances. People who have diversified income also experience the peace of not feeling trapped in their jobs and of not constantly being at the mercy of their employers. When you have multiple streams of income, you can breathe a lot easier knowing that if one stream dries up, other steady sources continue to come in.

How do you create multiple streams of income?

First, understand that there are three different types of income:

- **Earned income:** This comes from your labor. Small business income, W-2 income, commissioned sales income, and consulting income all fit into this category. Basically, anything that requires your labor is considered earned income. (Earned income is the highest taxed form of income.)
- **Portfolio income:** This income is generated through buying an investment and then reselling it at a higher cost. Some examples are buying and selling real estate, stocks, bonds, cars, trinkets, etc. (Typically, portfolio

income is taxed at a lower rate than earned income, depending on how long you hold the investment prior to selling it.)

- **Passive income:** This comes from any asset you have purchased or created, including rental income, business income that is not "earned" by your time and effort, book royalties, song royalties, and patent income, among others. Basically, passive income involves your work being done up front, but the payment for that work continuing to come in. With passive income, you are not working for money, but instead, your money is working for you. (Passive income is usually taxed at the lowest rates.)

All portfolio and passive income streams only come from three sources:

- Real Estate
- Paper Assets
- Your Own Business

We have a special report on this topic available on our website at www.ftmdaily.com. The special report is entitled, "15 Streams of Income That You Can Create Right Now!" Financial advisors currently say there are at least eleven streams of income a person can have in retirement. We have come up with fifteen in this special report.

While we have compiled a list of multiple streams of income, the list is really endless. The best types of income streams for you can be found by examining your hobbies and passions. Determine if there is a way to turn them into a steady stream of income.

The whole point of diversifying your income is to generate a number of different paychecks. As the U.S. economy continues to weaken, you will be glad you did.

ACTION STEP #7

Commit to adding another stream of income to your financial life in the next twelve months.

## Conclusion

I want to leave you with one final thought. As you have gathered from this book, the economic system of the United States of America is flawed in a number of ways. The reason the system is so imperfect is the nation's faulty financial foundation. Once you truly grasp the fatal flaws within the system, you may be tempted to become angry. This is especially true if you have a great patriotic love for America. Some may react to this new-found awareness by engaging in activism in the political and economic arenas. While I certainly do not want to discourage anyone from informing the public regarding the impending collapse of our nation's economy, I urge you to protect your own interests first—those of yourself and your family. If you have your entire house in order and have made adequate preparations, then I say debate to your heart's content. But for those who have not, now is not the time for debate. It is time to take action!

# About the Authors

## Terry James, General Editor

Terry James is author, general editor, and co-author of numerous books on Bible prophecy—hundreds of thousands of which have been sold worldwide. Some of his most recent titles include: *The American Apocalypse: Is the United States in Bible Prophecy?; The Nephilim Imperatives: Dark Sentences; The Rapture Dialogues: Dark Dimension* (foreword by Tim LaHaye); and *Are You Rapture Ready?* (foreword by Tim LaHaye).

James, a frequent lecturer on the study of end-time phenomena, is interviewed often by national and international media on topics involving world issues and events as they might relate to Bible prophecy. He has appeared in major documentaries and media forums in all media formats in America, Europe, and Asia. He currently appears as an expert source in a History Channel series entitled *The Nostradamus Effect*.

An active member of the Pre-Trib Research Center Study Group, James is a regular participant in the annual Tulsa Mid-America prophecy conference. He is also partner and general editor in the www.raptureready.com website, which is the attraction of national and international media and is rated as the number-one Bible prophecy website on the Internet.

## Tony Burtovoy II

Tony Burtovoy II, a husband and father of two, an avid sports fan, a golfer, an amateur gardener, and an amateur chef, serves as information systems manager for a mid-sized furniture and automotive parts manufacturer in America's Midwest. He's also a computer hobbyist and a big fan of Bible prophecy research. He finds nothing more satisfying than discovering new meanings to some of the Bible's old riddles. Self-described as "pretribulationist by nature but willing to wait, no matter how long it takes," he started researching prophecy subjects at age fifteen.

Many hours spent in bookstores and libraries early-on brought hard-fought-for information into view. The advent of the modern Internet in the early 1990s, along with his natural stubbornness, paved the way for an understanding of how the historical record fits with modern realities; he eventually found the answers to many of his early questions. He learned firsthand that an answer to one question can often lead to two or three new questions, and that with additional laborious study, prayer, and biblical review, one can easily find oneself deep into a journey that wasn't part of the original plan. But such is life sometimes, he believes—especially when in pursuit of the mysteries of the Lord.

## Barry J. Dyke

Barry James Dyke is president of Castle Asset Management LLC of Hampton, New Hampshire (www.castleassetmgmt.com). A financial planner for more than twenty-five years, he has founded a pension consulting business, a third-party administration firm, and a health and welfare consultancy. He is a registered investment advisor and has worked with individuals, privately held businesses, publicly traded companies, venture capital firms, and celebrities.

Dyke has written for and/or been written about in numerous publications, including *The Huffington Post, The New York Times, Advisor Today, The National Underwriter, Yahoo,* and *BusninessWeek.* He has been a frequent guest on talk radio shows throughout the country, and speaks to groups about conditions of today's economy and ways for consumers and advisors become better prepared in the days ahead. In 2009, more than one hundred thousand copies of his book, *The Pirates of Manhattan,* were purchased and distributed worldwide by some of the most well-respected and stable financial institutions in the country. The book illuminates corruption within the U.S. financial service industry and predicted the economic crisis early in 2007—months before it occurred.

For additional information, including press review copies, contact the author at barry@thepiratesofmanhattan.com or castleassetmgmt@comcast.net. Telephone is 603-929-7891 and mailing address is Castle Asset Management, LLC, 2 King's Highway, P.O. Box 95, Hampton, NH 03843-0095.Visit the author's website at www.thepiratesofmanhattan.com, or visit his new, award-winning blog at www.economicwarrior.org.

## Charles W. Gaines

Charles Gaines is a patent attorney and a shareholder of Hitt Gaines, P.C., an intellectual property law firm in Dallas. He holds multiple bachelor's degrees in chemistry and science education, and a doctorate in law. He is also trained in banking, finance, economics, and investments. He specializes in all facets of intellectual property law, with extensive experience in patent procurement in the chemical, materials science, optics, and mechanical arts. His expertise also includes preparing appeal briefs and arguments before courts of appeal, patentability, registrability, and infringement opinions as well as counseling corporations on intellectual property strategy, valuation, and cost control.

## G. Edward Griffin

G. Edward Griffin, a writer and documentary film producer, is listed in *Who's Who in America* and is well known because of his talent for researching difficult topics and presenting them in clear terms that all can understand. He has dealt with such diverse subjects as archaeology and ancient earth history, the Federal Reserve System and international banking, terrorism, internal subversion, the history of taxation, U.S. foreign policy, the science and politics of cancer therapy, the Supreme Court, and the United Nations. His better-known works include *The Creature from Jekyll Island, World without Cancer, The Discovery of Noah's Ark, Moles in High Places, The Open Gates of Troy, No Place to Hide, The Capitalist*

*Conspiracy, More Deadly than War, The Grand Design, The Great Prison Break,* and *The Fearful Master.*

Griffin is a graduate of the University of Michigan, where he majored in speech and communications. He also holds a Certified Financial Planner designation.

A recipient of the coveted Telly Award for excellence in television production, Griffin is the creator of the *Reality Zone Audio Archives* and president of American Media, a publishing and video production company in Southern California. He has served on the board of directors of the National Health Federation and the International Association of Cancer Victors and Friends. He is founder and president of the Coalition for Visible Ballots, the Cancer Cure Foundation, and Freedom Force International.

## C. H. Gruyère

C. H. Gruyère is no one of consequence. He is not even a voice crying or a finger pointing, just an echo of many voices who are concerned that we are at the end of the beginning of the end. Mr. Gruyère has been involved with the financial markets since 1982. He enjoys Swiss cheese.

## David H. Hitt

David Hitt is a patent attorney and a sharehololder of Hitt Gaines, P.C., an intellectual property law firm located in Dallas. He has bachelor's degrees in physics and accounting, a master's degree in taxation, and a doctorate in law. He is also formally educated

in economics, computer science, and mathematics. He specializes in all facets of intellectual property law, with extensive experience in patent procurement in the electrical, mechanical, and
computer arts, including: computer architectures; cryptography
and cryptanalysis; mathematical models of physical systems; tele-
communications systems; optical transmission systems; discrete
and integrated circuits; electromagnetic effects; control systems;
data security, recovery and forensics systems; land, air and space-
based military systems; motors and generators; turbo machinery;
hydraulic and pneumatic systems; fluid pumps, compressors and
motors; sensors and meters; thermal systems; and mechanical
transmissions and actuators. His expertise also includes preparing
patentability, registrability, and infringement opinions as well as
counseling corporations on intellectual property strategy, valuation, and cost control.

Mr. Hitt is also chairman of the board of Zola Levitt Ministries
and advises several other ministries on legal and technical matters.
He is a contributing author of *Flashpoint 2012* and is currently
writing a book on dimensionlessness.

## David W. Lowe

David W. Lowe graduated from Wichita State
University with a master's degree in professional
accounting, and is a certified public accountant
working in the field of corporate income tax. He resides with his
wife, Vivienne, in Wichita, KS, and together they teach an ele-
mentary age Sunday school class. Lowe is the author of two books
dealing with eschatology: *Earthquake Resurrection: Supernatural*

*Catalyst for the Coming Global Catastrophe* (2005) and *Then His Voice Shook the Earth: Mount Sinai, the Trumpet of God, and the Resurrection of the Dead in Christ* (2006). Visit Lowe's work online at his website, www.earthquakeresurrection.com.

## Jerry Robinson

Jerry Robinson is an economist, author, columnist, and international conference speaker. In addition, he hosts a weekly radio program entitled *Follow the Money Weekly*, an hour-long show dedicated to deciphering the week's top economic and financial news.

Robinson, who has appeared on numerous TV and radio programs—including FoxNews—to discuss global economic topics, is also author of the best-selling book, *Bankruptcy of Our Nation: 12 Key Strategies For Protecting Your Finances in These Uncertain Times* (New Leaf Press, 2009).

Recently, Robinson has been quoted by *USA Today* and other news agencies on the topic of the economy, and his columns have appeared regularly in numerous print and web publications, including *WorldNetDaily, Townhall,* and *FinancialSense*.

Robinson, who has spoken on the topics of money and economics around the globe, including the United States, Israel, Turkey, and Greece, is editor-in-chief of the popular economic newsletter, *Follow the Money Quarterly*. He resides in Texas with his beautiful wife.

## Todd Strandberg

Todd Strandberg is founder of www.rap-
tureready.com, the most highly visited prophecy
website on the Internet. He is partner in the site
with Terry James. The site has been written about in practically
every major news outlet in the nation and around the world.

Founded in 1987 when few websites existed, Rapture Ready
now commands the attention of a quarter million unique visi-
tors per month, with more than 13 million hits registered during
most thirty-day periods.

Strandberg is president of Rapture Ready and co-author of
*Are You Rapture Ready?*—a Penguin Group book under the E. P.
Dutton imprint. He has also written hundreds of major articles
for the Rapture Ready site, with many of those articles being
distributed in major publications and on websites around the
nation and world. He writes a highly read column under the site's
"Nearing Midnight" section, and created "The Rapture Index"—
a Dow Jones-like system of prophetic indicators that continues to
draw the attention of major news outlets.

# Notes

## Chapter One
### God's Economy *by David Lowe*

1   Wikipedia contributors, "Roman currency," *Wikipedia,*
    http://en.wikipedia.org/w/index.php?title=Roman_
    currency&oldid=412473822 (accessed February 21, 2011).

## Chapter Two
### Modern Money: Blind Faith and Bad Credit
*by Tony Burtovoy*

2   Wikipedia contributors, "John Dalberg-Acton, 1st Baron
    Acton," *Wikipedia,* http://en.wikipedia.org/w/index.
    php?title=John_Dalberg-Acton,_1st_Baron_Acton&oldid=417812740.
3   "Ponzi Schemes: Frequently Asked Questions," U. S. Securities and
    Exchange Commission, http://www.sec.gov/answers/ponzi.htm.
4   Ibid.
5   Wikipedia contributors, "Boom and Bust,"
    *Wikipedia,* http://en.wikipedia.org/w/index.
    php?title=Boom_and_bust&oldid=418042743.
6   "Fractional Banking," *The Jeremiah Project,* http://www.jeremiahproject.
    com/trashingamerica/fractional-banking.html.
7   Ibid.
8   Don Keko, "The Economic Collapse of the Roman Empire," *Examiner,*
    http://www.examiner.com/ancient-history-in-national/the-economic-
    collapse-of-the-roman-empire.
9   Wikipedia contributors, "Inflation in the Weimar
    Republic," *Wikipedia,* http://en.wikipedia.org/w/index.
    php?title=Inflation_in_the_Weimar_Republic&oldid=417230026.

10 "Benjamin Franklin," *Wikiquote,* http://en.wikiquote.
org/wiki/Benjamin_Franklin.

11 "Samuel Adams," *Quote DB,* http://www.quotedb.com/quotes/3590.

12 "Spirit of America Liberty Quotes," *USDOJ & Government Watch,*
http://www.dojgov.net/Liberty_Watch.htm.

## Chapter Three

**Banking: A Beast is Brought to Life** *by Charles W. Gaines*

13 "And that no man might buy or sell, save he that had the mark, or the
name of the beast, or the number of his name" (Revelation 13:17).

14 Wikipedia contributors, "History of Banking," *Wikipedia,* http://
en.wikipedia.org/wiki/History_of_banking (accessed January 23, 2011).

15 Ibid.

16 Ibid.

17 Ibid.

18 Ibid.

19 Bamber Gascoigne, *HistoryWorld,* from 2001, ongoing, http://www.
historyworld.net.

20 Ibid.

21 G. Edward Griffin, *The Creature from Jekyll Island,* 4th ed. (West Lake
Village: American Media, 2002).

22 *American Heritage Dictionary.*

23 "Are My Deposits Insured?" *FDIC,* http://www.fdic.gov/deposit/deposits
(accessed February 10, 2011).

24 Ibid.

25 "$250,000 Share Insurance Protection Extended to 2013," *National
Credit Union Administration,* http://www.ncua.gov/news/press_
releases/2009/MR09-0526.htm (accessed February 10, 2011).

26 "About BIS," *Bank for International Settlements,* http://www.bis.org/
about/index.htm.

27 Wikipedia contributors, "Bank of International Settlements," *Wikipedia,*
http://en.wikipedia.org/wiki/Bank_for_International_Settlements
(January 24, 2011).

28 Ibid.

29 Richard F. O'Brien. *Global Financial Integration: The End of Geography*
(New York: Counsel for Foreign Relations Press, 1992).

30 Arthur Sullivan and Steven M. Sheffrin, *Economics: Principles in Action*
(Upper Saddle River, New Jersey 07458: Pearson Prentice Hall) 254,

http://www.pearsonschool.com/index.cfm?locator=PSZ3R9&PMDbSite
Id=2781&PMDbSolutionId=6724&PMDbCategoryId=&PMDbProgr
amId=12881&level=4.

31 "Central Bank," *Britannica Online Encyclopedia*, http://www.britannica.
com/EBchecked/topic/102342/central-bank (accessed November 2,
2010).

32 Wikipedia contributors, "Central Bank," *Wikipedia*, http://en.wikipedia.
org/wiki/Central_bank (accessed February 1, 2011).

33 "The Structure of the Federal Reserve System," *Federal Reserve
Education*, http://federalreserveeducation.org/about-the-fed/structure-
and-functions/ (retrieved October 1, 2010).

34 See generally, Griffin.

35 Eustace Mullins, *Secrets of the Federal Reserve* (Staunton, Va.: Bankers
Research Institute, 1983).

36 *Board of Governors of the Federal Reserve System*, March 7, 2007, http://
www.federalreserve.gov/generalinfo/faq/faqfrs.htm.

37 Neil Irwin, "Federal Reserve Earned $45 Billion in 2009,"
*Washington Post*, http://www.washingtonpost.com/wp-dyn/content/
article/2010/01/11/AR2010011103892.html (accessed January 12,
2010).

38 Stephen Zarlenga, "Is the Federal Reserve System a Governmental or a
Privately Controlled Organization?" *American Monetary Institute*, July 8,
2008, http://www.monetary.org/federalreserveprivate.htm.

39 See generally, Griffin.

40 Zarlenga.

41 Robert DeYoung and Tara Rice, "How Do Banks Make Money?" *Federal
Reserve Bank of Chicago*, 4Q 2004, http//www.chicagofed.org.

42 See generally, Griffin.

43 A full explanation of this concept is outside the scope of this chapter.
However, one can read more on this topic in Griffin, noted above.

44 "The Federal Discount Rate," www.Bankrate.com (accessed February
10, 2011).

45 David Jeremiah, *The Coming Economic Armageddon* (New York:
FaithWords, 2010).

46 "EconomyWatch," *World GDP,* http://www.economywatch.com/gdp/
world-gdp (accessed February 13, 2011).

47 Jeremiah.

48 DeYoung and Rice.

49 Ibid.

50  Paul Solman, "Unraveling the Profit Puzzle at Goldman
    Sachs," *PBS News Hour,* February 11, 2010, http://www.pbs.
    org/newshour/bb/business/jan-june10/goldmansachs_02-11.html.

51  Stevenson Jacobs, "Bank of America 2Q Profit Jumps 15 Percent,"
    *Huffington Post,* July 16, 2010, http://www.huffingtonpost.
    com/2010/07/16/bank-of-america-2q-profit_n_648970.html (accessed
    February 9, 2011).

52  David Widener, "Why Banks (Still) Aren't Lending," *MSN Market
    Watch,* April 23, 2009, http://articles.moneycentral.msn.com/Investing/
    Extra/why-banks-still-are-not-lending.aspx.

53  *FDIC,* http://www2.fdic.gov/hsob/HSOBSummaryRpt.asp?BegYear=19
    34&EndYear=2007&State=1, (accessed February 9, 2011).

54  Wikipedia contributors, "2008–2011 Bank Failures in the
    United States," *Wikipedia,* http://en.wikipedia.org/wiki/
    2008%E2%80%932010_bank_failures_in_the_United_States (accessed
    January 23, 2011).

55  Ibid.

56  Martin Weiss, "Shocking New Failures Possible in the U.S.
    and Overseas," *Money and Markets,* January 31, 2011, www.
    moneyandmarkets.com.

## Chapter Five

### The Revolving Door: Between Bankers, Politicians, the Federal Reserve, Lobbyists, and Ivy-League Academia

*by Barry James Dyke*

57  Back stops are taxpayer-subsidized loss arrangements in which the
    government agrees to absorb financial losses on investments after
    a certain breakpoint. For instance, after $1 billion in losses, the
    government could agree to pay 80 or 100 percent of the loss after the $1
    billion—like an insurance deductible.

58  A fund-of-fund hedge-fund is made up of multiple, various hedge funds;
    a hybrid of many.

## Chapter Six
### Economic Slavery *by Todd Strandberg*

59 Laura Brace, *The Politics of Property, Labour, Freedom, and Belonging* (Edinburgh, Scotland: Edinburgh University, 2004), http://books. google.co.uk/books?id=osZnIiqDd4sC&pg=PA162.

60 Wikipedia contributors, "Racism in Africa," *Wikipedia,* http://en.wikipedia.org/w/index.php?title=Racism_in_ Africa&oldid=416893610 (accessed March 8, 2011).

61 David Reagan, "The Love of Money: The Root of All Evil or All Kinds of Evil?" *Learn the Bible,* http://www.learnthebible.org/the-love-of-money-root-of-all-evil-or-all-kinds-of-evil.html.

62 Craig R. Smith, "True Wealth: The Historical Battle over Money," *True Wealth: Sound Economic Solutions,* http://www.true-wealth.com/content/cpt2/his_batt.htm.

63 Bethany Winkel, "Alcohol Abuse Among Native Americans," *Treatment Solutions Network,* December 17, 2010, http://www.treatmentsolutionsnetwork.com/blog/index. php/2010/12/17/alcohol-abuse-among-native-americans/.

64 Eric Newhouse, "Bane of the Blackfeet," *Great Falls Tribune,* August 22, 1999, http://www.pulitzer.org/archives/6337.

65 Jerry Price, "Racial Reconciliation—Native Americans," *The Ethics and Religious Liberty Commission of the Southern Baptist Convention,* February 6, 2006, http://erlc.com/article/racial-reconciliation-native-americans/.

66 Newhouse.

67 "Who Gets Welfare?" *Ebony,* December 1992, http://findarticles. com/p/articles/mi_m1077/is_n2_v48/ai_12970819/.

68 Violence Policy Center, "Black Homicide Victimization in the United States: An Analysis of 2007 Data," January 2010, .http://www.vpc.org/studies/blackhomicide10.pdf.

69 Lloyd Marcus, "Diversity on Tea Party Express," *Lloyd Marcus,* March 31, 2010, http://www.lloydmarcus.com/?m=201003.

70 M. Catharine Evans, "Sharpton and Obama Ignore Planned Parenthood's Racist Underbelly," *American Thinker,* February 28, 2011, http://www.americanthinker. com/2011/02/sharpton_and_obama_ignore_plan_1.html.

71 Tyler Durden, "Marc Faber: 'I Think We Are All Doomed,'" *The Market Guardian,* February 27, 2011, http://www.themarketguardian. com/2011/02/marc-faber-i-think-we-are-all-doomed/.

72   "Average Interest Rates, January," *Treasury Direct,* January 2011, http://www.treasurydirect.gov/govt/rates/pd/avg/2011/2011_01.htm.

73   Wikipedia contributors, "Reserve currency," *Wikipedia, The Free Encyclopedia,* http://en.wikipedia.org/w/index.php?title=Reserve_currency&oldid=414263854.

## Chapter Seven

### Economic Collapse: What a Difference a Day Makes

*by Tony Burtovoy II*

74   Pater Tenebrarum, "The Problem of Fractional Reserve Banking," *Acting Man,* July 5, 2010, http://www.acting-man.com/?p=3723 (emphasis added).

75   Wikipedia contributors, "Inflation in the Weimar Republic," *Wikipedia,* http://en.wikipedia.org/w/index.php?title=Inflation_in_the_Weimar_Republic&oldid=411592257 (emphasis added).

76   Ibid.

77   Ibid.

78   Wikipedia contributors, "Hyperinflation," *Wikipedia,* http://en.wikipedia.org/w/index.php?title=Hyperinflation&oldid=415646215.

79   Thayer Watkins, "The Worst Episode of Hyperinflation in History: Yugoslavia 1993–94," *Roger Sherman Society,* http://www.rogershermansociety.org/yugoslavia.htm.

80   Ibid.

81   Wikipedia contributors, "1998 Russian financial crisis," *Wikipedia,* http://en.wikipedia.org/w/index.php?title=1998_Russian_financial_crisis&oldid=412691033.

82   Ibid.

83   Ibid.

84   Wikipedia contributors, "Hyperinflation in Zimbabwe," *Wikipedia,* http://en.wikipedia.org/w/index.php?title=Hyperinflation_in_Zimbabwe&oldid=415974599.

85   Ibid.

86   Ibid.

87   Ibid.

88   Ibid.

89 Eva Cheng, "Argentina: What Caused the World's Largest Default?" February 6, 2002, *Green Left Weekly,* http://www.greenleft.org. au/node/25980.
90 Ibid.
91 Ibid.

## Chapter Eight

### Stock Markets: A Casino without Comps *by C. H. Gruyère*

92 Robert Lenzner, "Why Isn't Angelo Mozilo in Jail?" "Streettalk," in *Forbes,* October 16, 2010, http://blogs.forbes. com/robertlenzner/2010/10/16/why-isnt-angelo-mozillo-in-jail/.
93 "Derivatives: The Quadrillion Dollar Financial Casino Completely Dominated by the Big International Banks," *The Economic Collapse,* December 13, 2010, http://theeconomiccollapseblog.com/archives/ derivatives-the-quadrillion-dollar-financial-casino-completely-dominated-by-the-big-international-banks.
94 Jim Rawles, "Derivatives—The Mystery Man Who'll Break the Global Bank at Monte Carlo," September 25, 2006, *Survival Blog,* http://www.survivalblog.com/cgi-bin/mt43/mt-search. cgi?search=triggered+by+the+popping&IncludeBlogs=2&limit=20.

## Chapter Nine

### Satan's Economy: The Inescapable, Predestined Endgame

*by Terry James*

95 Wilfred Hahn, *Eternal Value Review,* April 2011, www.eternalvalue.com.
96 As quoted in *New York Times,* October 28, 1973.
97 George Santayana, *The Life of Reason or the Phases of Human Progress* (New York: Scribner's, 1954), 82.
98 Lord Edward Acton, in a letter written to Mandel Creighton, April 3, 1887.
99 Middle East and North African revolution timeline sources include the following: Reuters, *Los Angeles Times,* BBC, *The Guardian,* CNN International, *The New York Times,* AFP, www.wsj.com.